Praise for *Agile Product Management with Scrum*

"Product owners have had few places to turn to for advice, despite having the hardest role on an agile project. This book rectifies that. Roman Pichler's insights into the duties of the product owner are powerful and practical. Correctly applied, his advice will benefit any product owner and agile team."
— Mike Cohn, Author of *Succeeding with Agile, Agile Estimating and Planning,* and *User Stories Applied*

"Scrum is silent on how a product owner can maximize value. Most product managers and marketers don't know how to use the iterative, incremental nature of Scrum to do so. Roman has filled this hole nicely with his new book, *Agile Product Management with Scrum.*"
— Ken Schwaber, codeveloper of the Scrum process

"With so little written on the intersections of agile methods and product management, Roman makes a significant contribution to the field. The book provides clear guidance and rich examples on how to become an agile product manager and a successful product owner, and, further, how to lead with a strong vision. This book is a must read for product managers new to Scrum, product owners new to product management, and any product manager who wants to get the most out of Agile."
— Greg Cohen, Principal Consultant, 280 Group and Director, Silicon Valley Product Management Association

"I'm always happy to hear what Roman is thinking. What I really like about this book is that he not only shares his experience ("Common Mistakes" is a great section), but he also brings in the wisdom of others in the field. This powerful combination allows him to see farther ahead and share that vision with us. Thanks, Roman!"
— Linda Rising, Independent Consultant and coauthor of *Fearless Change: Patterns for Introducing New Ideas*

"Roman Pichler's new and remarkable book focuses on the product and the product owner role, applying Scrum to the whole value chain. His experience as a coach leads to genuinely balanced, practical, and applicable solutions for every conceivable situation in the product lifecycle. This is the definitive reference guide to agile product management for all practitioners!"
— Markus Andrezak, Manager, Outsourced Product Development, mobile.international GmbH

"Roman Pichler's product owner book is an easy-to-read and comprehensive description of the important role of the product owner in Scrum. It points out the significance of vision and leadership, as well as minimal marketable products and short release cycles. It is a resource for new product owners to get into their job and gives management good advice on choosing the right person for that job."
— Andrea Heck, Dipl-Inf (Univ.), Agile Transition Project Manager

"The product owner is a vital role in Scrum, and Roman's new book is a welcome contribution to helping product owners succeed."
— Craig Larman, coauthor of *Scaling Lean & Agile Development* and *Practices for Scaling Lean & Agile Development*

"Roman's no-nonsense approach takes Scrum back to its roots, examining and building on the fundamental concepts behind product ownership. The focus on teamwork is a welcome antidote to process-centric views of Scrum, showing how the product owner role changes and challenges the status quo of the traditionally run project. Well-researched, Roman leverages both his own experience as well as that of others, clearly showing how Scrum product ownership works to solve common problems, citing real-world examples of both success and failure. Scattered with practical tips, this book is for anybody who wants to manage or to be a Scrum product owner and release successful products using Scrum."

—Simon Bennett, Global Competency Lead and Product Owner,
EMC Consulting

"Roman Pichler's *Agile Product Management with Scrum* is destined to be a vital reference for agile product managers, product owners, business analysts, and anybody wanting to be a great agile product manager. Roman shares practical tips and guidance on all aspects of agile planning, the care and feeding of your product backlog, and the essential activities of visioning, valuing, and collaborating. *Agile Product Management with Scrum* will raise your awareness of the complex, multifaceted discipline of agile product management. Better yet, all agile team members will benefit by reading this book, because on every successful agile team, we all think like product managers."

—Ellen Gottesdiener, President/Founder, EBG Consulting, Inc.

"Agile software development is about incrementally converting requirements into working software using short iterations. *Agile Product Management with Scrum* answers one of the most important questions in product organizations: "Are we building the right product?" Or, as Roman so passionately put it in his subtitle, *Creating Products that Customers Love*. Roman's book is the long-awaited link to turn a broad vision into meaningful and digestible requirements. It provides a thorough introduction to the Scrum framework for product managers and executives who are eager to reduce development costs and time-to-market delivery of exciting new software products."

—Jochen Krebs, Incrementor and Author of *Agile Portfolio Management*

"Roman delivers an agile product management book that clearly describes the importance, challenges, and pitfalls of the product owner role. Using practical examples, highlighting common mistakes, and supplying reflection questions at the end of each chapter, Roman makes the role of product owner easily accessible and doable. This is the book to read for any organization wishing to implement Scrum."

—Jessica Hildrum, former CEO of Norway's premier Agile training company

"At the core of every successful agile development team is a visionary, engaged, and empowered product manager. In *Agile Product Management with Scrum*, Roman Pichler gives us a simple, no-nonsense definition of the role that will lead any Scrum team to amazing results. For all of you that want to get under the covers of the most important role in agile development, this is the book for you. A must for every new product owner!"

—Steve Greene, Vice President, Program Management & Agile Development,
salesforce.com

Agile Product Management with Scrum

Agile Product Management with Scrum

Creating Products that Customers Love

Roman Pichler

✦✦ Addison-Wesley

Upper Saddle River, NJ • Boston • Indianapolis • San Francisco
New York • Toronto • Montreal • London • Munich • Paris • Madrid
Capetown • Sydney • Tokyo • Singapore • Mexico City

Many of the designations used by manufacturers and sellers to distinguish their products are claimed as trademarks. Where those designations appear in this book, and the publisher was aware of a trademark claim, the designations have been printed with initial capital letters or in all capitals.

The author and publisher have taken care in the preparation of this book, but make no expressed or implied warranty of any kind and assume no responsibility for errors or omissions. No liability is assumed for incidental or consequential damages in connection with or arising out of the use of the information or programs contained herein.

The publisher offers excellent discounts on this book when ordered in quantity for bulk purchases or special sales, which may include electronic versions and/or custom covers and content particular to your business, training goals, marketing focus, and branding interests. For more information, please contact:

U.S. Corporate and Government Sales
(800) 382-3419
corpsales@pearsontechgroup.com

For sales outside the United States please contact:

International Sales
international@pearsoned.com

Visit us on the Web: informit.com/aw

Library of Congress Cataloging-in-Publication Data

Pichler, Roman.
 Agile product management with Scrum : creating products that customers love /
Roman Pichler.
   p. cm.
 Includes bibliographical references and index.
 ISBN 978-0-321-60578-8 (pbk. : alk. paper)
 1. Agile software development. 2. Scrum (Computer software development) I. Title.
 QA76.76.D47P494 2010
 005.1—dc22

                                                                    2010000751

Pearson Education, Inc.
Rights and Contracts Department
501 Boylston Street, Suite 900
Boston, MA 02116
Fax: (617) 671-3447

ISBN-13: 978-0-321-60578-8
ISBN-10:   0-321-60578-0
Text printed in the United States on recycled paper at LSC Communications, Crawfordsville.
ScoutAutomatedPrintCode

To Melissa

CONTENTS

FOREWORD
BY JEFF SUTHERLAND

The product owner is a new role for most companies and needs this book's compelling and easily understandable presentation. When the first product owner was selected, I was a vice president at Object Technology, responsible for delivering the first product created by Scrum. The new product would make or break the company, and I had six months to deliver a development tool that would alter the market. In addition to creating the product with a small, carefully selected team, I had to organize the whole company around new product delivery. With only a few months until product shipment, it was clear that the right minimal feature set would determine success or failure. I found that I did not have enough time to spend talking with customers and watching competitors closely so that I could precisely determine the right prioritized feature set up front and break those features down into small product backlog items for the team.

I had already delegated my engineering responsibilities to the first ScrumMaster, John Scumniotales, but now I needed a product owner. I had access to any resource in the company, so I selected the best person from the product management team for the role I had in mind: Don Roedner. As the first product owner, Don had to own the vision for the product, the business plan and the revenue, the road map and the release plan, and, most important, a carefully groomed and precisely prioritized product backlog for the team.

Don lived with the team half of his time and was on the road with customers the other half. His job was to deliver the right product, while I worked with the entire company on product naming and branding, marketing strategy and communications, and sales planning and training while simultaneously sitting in the Scrum meeting every day and being the primary impediment remover for the team. Don had to assume a bigger role than product marketing manager. All of a sudden he owned a new line of business. At the same time he was plunged into the engineering team, helping to explain and motivate the team on a daily basis. Being embedded in the market and embedded in the team at the same time was a total immersion experience.

A good product owner's intensity of focus and responsibility for success are clearly illustrated in this book but rarely seen in product companies or on IT teams. We need a compelling picture of a great product owner along with the specifics of how to execute the role, and Roman Pichler has provided an outstanding guide.

Jeff Sutherland,
Cocreator of Scrum

FOREWORD
BY BRETT QUEENER

There is a great movement taking place today throughout the software industry: the agile movement. Over the last two decades, many customers, partners, and employees have become disenchanted with the way we develop enterprise technology solutions. These solutions are often low in quality, take years to be brought to market, and lack the innovation necessary to solve real business problems.

At Salesforce.com, we aspire to be a different software company by focusing on customer and employee success. We knew that using traditional methods to deliver software just wouldn't work for our vision of a different kind of company. We had to rethink the model, throw out our assumptions, and find a better way. We asked ourselves: Is there a way to deliver high-quality software on time, every time? Is there a way to get value into our customers' hands early and often? Is there a way to innovate at scale as the company grows? In fact, there is.

As the chief product owner at Salesforce.com, I needed a way for my product managers to effectively connect the wants and needs of our customers and the business directly to the development teams in a highly dynamic and responsive way. Using Scrum allows us to put the product managers firmly in charge of delivering customer value. It enables them to direct the team to build the most business-critical features first and to get them into the hands of our customers as soon as possible. It also provides them with the flexibility to respond quickly to changing market conditions and competitive pressures, or to deliver terrific new innovations emerging from our development teams. In *Agile Product Management with Scrum*, you'll see how a product owner differs from a traditional product manager having a greater level of responsibility for the success of the product. The book clearly outlines and contrasts the different behaviors between the traditional and the agile role.

Many have attempted to explain the product owner role, but none have been able to capture the essence of the role like Roman Pichler. This book offers compelling agile product management theories and practices that guide product owners, Scrum team members, and executives in delivering innovations. Roman provides plenty of real-world examples from highly competitive innovators like Salesforce.com along with simple explanations for building and delivering the minimum functionality to deliver innovations. He also outlines the common pitfalls and mistakes that many product owners make.

In today's dynamic and competitive environment, our customers' expectations and demands are greater than ever before. At Salesforce.com, our agile approach has provided dramatic results with our product owners delivering more innovation and value. If you're interested in similar success, this book is for you. The spot-on tools, techniques, and advice are the perfect guide to deliver wild success for your customers.

Brett Queener,
Senior Vice President, Products, Salesforce.com

PREFACE

Many excellent books have been written on agile software development and on product management. Yet to date, a comprehensive description of how product management works in an agile context does not exist. It is as if agilists have shied away from the subject, and the product management experts are still scratching their heads trying to figure out this brave new agile world. With more and more companies adopting Scrum, the question of how product management is practiced in a Scrum environment is becoming increasingly urgent. This book attempts to provide an answer.

When I first came across agile practices in 1999, I was struck by the close collaboration between business and technical people. Until then, I had considered software development as something techies would take an interest in but not businesspeople. When I coached my first agile project in 2001, the biggest challenge was to help the product mangers transition into the agile world. Since then, product ownership has consistently been the major challenge and success factor in the companies I've consulted—not only in developing successful products but also in making Scrum stick. To say it with the words of Chris Fry and Steve Greene (2007, 139), who guided the agile transition at Salesforce.com:

Throughout our initial rollout we heard from many experts that the Product Owner role was key to the success of our agile transformation. Although we intuitively understood this we didn't truly understand the significant changes that the Product Owners would experience in their roles.

WHY AGILE PRODUCT MANAGEMENT IS DIFFERENT

Scrum-based agile product management differs from old-school product management approaches in a number of areas. Table P.1 provides a summary of the most important distinctions.[1]

TABLE P.1 Old-School versus New-School Product Management

Old School	New School
Several roles, such as product marketer, product manager, and project manager, share the responsibility for bringing the product to life.	One person—the product owner—is in charge of the product and leads the project. Find out more about this new role in Chapter 1 and Chapter 6.
Product managers are detached from the development teams, separated by process, department, and facility boundaries.	The product owner is a member of the Scrum team and works closely with the ScrumMaster and team on an ongoing basis. Find out more in Chapter 1, Chapter 3, and Chapter 5.
Extensive market research, product planning, and business analysis are carried out up front.	Minimum up-front work is expended to create a vision that describes what the product will roughly look like and do, as discussed in Chapter 2.

---

1. Note that I use the Scrum role names stated in Schwaber (2009).

TABLE P.1 Old-School versus New-School Product Management *(Continued)*

Old School	New School
Up-front product discovery and definition: requirements are detailed and frozen early on.	Product discovery is an ongoing process; requirements emerge. There is no definition phase and no market or product requirements specification. The product backlog is dynamic, and its contents evolve based on customer and user feedback. Find out more in Chapter 3.
Customer feedback is received late, in market testing and after product launch.	Early and frequent releases together with sprint review meetings generate valuable customer and user feedback that helps create a product customers love, as discussed in Chapter 4 and Chapter 5.

Agile methods including Scrum embrace an age-old truth: They see change as the only constant. "If a company's own research does not make a product obsolete, another's will," wrote Theodore Levitt famously in his article "Marketing Myopia," published in 1960. And Christensen (1997) argues that disruptive innovation will eventually occur in every industry. Only how soon and how frequently it is going to happen remain uncertain. Companies not able to adapt quickly will go out of business—even if their profits are healthy today. Luckily, Scrum's empirical nature makes it well suited to deal with newness and innovation, to cope with complex situations where flux and unpredictability are dominant forces. If your business is characterized by change, you are likely to find a powerful ally in Scrum.

WHAT THIS BOOK OFFERS AND WHO SHOULD READ IT

This book is for anyone interested in agile product management, particularly those readers working as product owners or transitioning into the role. The book discusses the role of the product owner along with essential product management practices. These include envisioning the product, stocking and grooming the product backlog, planning and tracking the release, leveraging the Scrum meetings, and transitioning into the new role. This practical guide enables you to apply agile product management techniques effectively in Scrum. It focuses on products involving software—from a simple software application to complex products like mobile phones.

Note that this book is not a product management primer. It is not a Scrum primer, either. And it certainly is no product management panacea. In fact, there are many product management aspects this book does not cover. Instead, this book focuses on the product management concepts and practices specific to Scrum.

The book assumes that you are familiar with Scrum and that you have a working product management knowledge. A description of Scrum can be found in Schwaber and Beedle (2002) and Schwaber (2004).

My hope is that this book will help you create products that customers love—products that are beneficial to their users and are developed in a healthy, sustainable way.

ACKNOWLEDGMENTS

This book has been shaped by the contributions of many people. I'd like to wholeheartedly thank everyone who reviewed chapters, shared stories, or provided advice (in alphabetical order):

Lyssa Adkins, Geir Amsjø, Markus Andrezak, Gabrielle Benefield, Robert Bogetti, Thomke Buhl, Marty Cagan, Sabine Canditt, John Clifford, Alistair Cockburn, Mike Cohn, Jens Coldeway, Kaustabh Debbarman, Pete Deemer, Chris Fry, Steve Greene, Roland Hanbury, Kevlin Henney, Ben Hogan, Clinton Keith, Andreas Klinger, Hans-Peter Korn, Jochen Krebs, Craig Larman, Bill Li, Lowell Lindstrom, Catherine Louis, Rodrigo Luna, Artem Marchenko, Jason Martinez, Ralph Miarka, Philip Missler, Bent Myllerup, Jeff Patton, Tobias Pichler, Brett Queener, Cesário Ramos, Dan Rawsthorne, Simon Roberts, Stefan Roock, Rene Rosendahl, Johanna Rothman, Kenneth Rubin, Martin Rusnak, Hans-Peter Samios, Bob Schatz, Andreas Schliep, Ken Schwaber, Christa Schwanninger, Karl Scotland, Martin Shaw, Lisa Shoop, James Siddle, Michele Sliger, Preston Smith, Dieter Stefanowitz, Jeff Sutherland, Mads Troels Hansen, Bas Vodde, Geoff Watts, Harvey Wheaton, Rüdiger Wolf, Elizabeth Woodward, and Lv Yi.

I am particularly grateful to Mike Cohn. Mike's patient shepherding, help, and ongoing feedback were invaluable in writing this book. Thank you very much, Mike! Special thanks to Jeff Sutherland and Brett Queener for writing such great forewords. And thank you, Ken Schwaber, for teaching me Scrum.

I am forever grateful to my family. My wife, Melissa Pichler, gave me the time and focus to write the book, and she discussed ideas with me, reviewed the chapters, and helped with the cover design. Thanks, honey! Thank you also to my son, Leo, and my daughter, Yasmin, for tiptoeing around (or trying to) when Daddy was writing his book. Special thanks to Leo, age five, for providing honest feedback after reading a few sentences of the book: "Daddy, it's a bit weird."

I would also like to thank Rebecca Traeger for her excellent editorial work and the team at Pearson—Chris Guzikowski, Raina Chrobak, Sheri Cain, Anna Popick, and Barbara Wood—for all their help and hard work.

ABOUT THE AUTHOR

Roman Pichler is a leading Scrum and agile product management expert. He has a long track record in teaching and coaching product owners and in helping companies apply effective product management practices. In addition to this book, he is the bestselling author of *Scrum—Agiles Projektmanagement erfolgreich einsetzen* (*Scrum—Applying Agile Project Management Successfully*). Roman is a frequent speaker at international conferences. As a Certified Scrum Trainer, he led the Scrum Alliance effort to develop a curriculum for the Certified Scrum Product Owner training. Find out more at www.romanpichler.com.

1
· · ·
UNDERSTANDING THE PRODUCT
OWNER ROLE

I once worked on a new health-care product destined to replace its predecessor. The new system was intended to provide more value for the customers and leapfrog the competition. After over two years of development, the new product was launched with great expectations—and bombed.

What went wrong? Somewhere between the idea and the launch, the product vision was lost amid the many handoffs. Product marketing performed the market research, wrote the product concept, and passed the concept on to the product manager. The product manager wrote the requirements specification and handed it off to the project manager, who passed it on to the development teams. There was no single person responsible for leading the effort to create a winning product, and no shared vision of what the product should look like and do. Everyone involved had a different view, a different vision.

What's the solution? Putting one person, called the product owner, in charge of the product. This chapter explores the role of the product owner. It explains the role's authority and responsibility as well as how the role should be applied.

THE PRODUCT OWNER ROLE

In the "Scrum Guide" (Schwaber 2009, 5), Ken Schwaber writes about the product owner:

> The Product Owner is the one and only person responsible for managing the Product Backlog and ensuring the value of the work the team performs. This person maintains the Product Backlog and ensures that it is visible to everyone.

This definition sounds rather harmless until we consider its implications. The product owner leads the development effort to create a product that generates the desired benefits. This often includes creating the product vision; grooming the product backlog; planning the release; involving customers, users, and other stakeholders; managing the budget; preparing the product launch; attending the Scrum meetings; and collaborating with the team. The product owner plays a crucial part not only in bringing new products to life but also in managing the product lifecycle. Having one person in charge across releases ensures continuity and reduces handoffs, and it encourages long-term thinking. A survey at SAP AG revealed more benefits: The employees working as product owners felt more confident, more able to influence, more visible, better organized, and better motivated in the new role (Schmidkonz 2008).

Being the product owner is no solo act. The product owner is part of the Scrum team and closely collaborates with its other members. While the ScrumMaster and team support the product owner by jointly grooming the product backlog, the product owner is responsible for making sure that the necessary work is carried out.

It may be tempting to compare the role of the product owner to traditional roles, such as product manager or project manager. Any comparison fails to do it justice, though. The product owner is a new, multifaceted role that unites the authority and responsibility traditionally scattered across separate roles, including the customer or sponsor, the product manager, and the project manager. Its specific shape is context-sensitive: It depends on the nature of the product, the stage of the product lifecycle, and the size of the project, among other factors. For example, the product owner responsible for a new product consisting of software, hardware, and mechanics will need different competencies than one who is leading the effort to enhance a web application. Similarly, a product owner working with a large Scrum project will require different skills than one collaborating with only one or two teams.

For commercial products, the product owner is typically a customer representative, such as a product manager or marketer. An actual customer tends to assume the role when the product is being developed for a specific organization, for instance, an external client who requires a new data warehouse solution or an internal client (e.g., the marketing department) asking for a web site update. I have worked with customers, users, business line managers, product managers, project managers, business analysts, and architects who filled the product owner role well in the given circumstances. Even CEOs can play the product owner role. Take the example of Ript, a visual planning tool that lets users cut and paste images and text from one application to another. The software was the brainchild of Gerry Laybourne, CEO of Oxygen Media, who subsequently took on the product owner role for the software's first release (Judy 2007).

DESIRABLE CHARACTERISTICS OF A PRODUCT OWNER

Choosing the right product owner is crucial for any Scrum project. Successful product owners I have worked with share the characteristics that follow. Since the product owner is a new role, individuals often need time and support to transition into the role and to acquire the necessary skills. A common challenge is finding employees with the necessary breadth and depth of knowledge and experience to do the job well. (I'll discuss transitioning to the role and developing product owners in Chapter 6.)

Visionary and Doer

Writer Jonathan Swift observed, "Vision is the art of seeing things invisible." The product owner is a visionary who can envision the final product and communicate the vision. The product owner is also a doer who sees the vision through to completion. This includes describing requirements, closely collaborating with the team, accepting or rejecting work results, and steering the project by tracking and forecasting its progress. As an entrepreneur, the product owner facilitates creativity; encourages innovation; and is comfortable with change, ambiguity, debate, conflict, playfulness, experimentation, and informed risk taking.

Leader and Team Player

"Good business leaders create a vision, articulate the vision, passionately own the vision, and relentlessly drive it to completion," says Jack Welch, GE's former chairman and CEO. The product owner is just such a leader. As the individual responsible for the product's success, the product owner provides guidance and direction for everyone involved in the development effort and ensures that tough decisions are made. For instance, should the launch date be postponed or should less functionality be delivered? At the same time, the product owner must be a team player who relies on close collaboration with the other Scrum team members, yet has no formal authority over them. We can think of the product owner as *primus inter pares*, first among peers, regarding the product.

The dual nature of the product owner as a leader and team player is a hard line to toe. By no means should the product owner dictate decisions, yet at the same time neither should the product owner be indecisive or employ a laissez-faire management style.

Instead, the individual should act as a shepherd for the innovation process, guiding the project and seeking team consensus in the decision-making process. Making decisions about the product collaboratively ensures the team's buy-in, leverages the team's creativity and knowledge, and results in better decisions. Working this way requires facilitation and patience because team members often have to disagree and argue first before a new solution can be synthesized from the different ideas and perspectives. Kaner and his coauthors provide useful information on collaborative decision making and related facilitation techniques (1996).

The Entrepreneurial Team

We sometimes focus on an individual as the amazing entrepreneur or the outstanding leader—think of Bill Gates, Steve Jobs, and other celebrity leaders. In reality, very few innovations are a stroke of genius attained by one person. And even if the product owner is Mrs. or Mr. Innovation, the individual still needs a team to bring the product to life. No entrepreneurial genius can make all the right decisions. In fact, neuroscientific research reveals that even the best-qualified person in the right job at the right place can make wrong decisions—if that person decides alone. Finkelstein and his coauthors attribute this to the way human cognition works (2009). They recommend using at least one other person as a sounding board. A team provides plenty of sparring partners to test ideas and arrive at the right decision. Ed Catmull, president of Pixar (2008, 68), says this:

> ... if you give a mediocre idea to a great team, they will either fix it or throw it away and come up with something that works.

The wisdom of many is preferable to the brilliance of one.

Communicator and Negotiator

The product owner must be an effective communicator and negotiator. The individual communicates with and aligns different parties, including customers, users, development and engineering, marketing, sales, service, operations, and management. The product owner is the voice of the customer, communicating customer needs and requirements and bridging the gap between "the suits" and "the techies." Sometimes this means saying no and other times negotiating a compromise.

Empowered and Committed

The product owner must have enough authority and the right level of management sponsorship to lead the development effort and to align stakeholders. At mobile.de, Germany's biggest online auto marketplace, senior management selects product owners, provides support, and acts as their escalation partner. This close collaboration has allowed the management team to better understand the progress of the individual projects and to kill unsuccessful projects early.[1]

An empowered product owner is essential for leading the effort to bring the product to life. The product owner must have the proper decision-making authority—from finding the right team members to deciding which functionality is delivered as part of the release. The product owner must be someone who can be entrusted with a budget and at the same time has the ability to create a work environment that fosters creativity and innovation. The product owner must be committed to the development effort. A successful product owner is confident, enthusiastic, energetic, and trustworthy.

Available and Qualified

The product owner must be available and qualified to do a great job. Being the product owner is usually a full-time job. It is important to give product owners enough time to sustainably carry out their responsibilities. If the individual is overworked, the project's progress suffers and the resulting product may be suboptimal.

---

1. Personal communication with Philip Missler, CTO at mobile.de, June 18, 2009.

Being adequately qualified usually requires an intimate understanding of the customer and the market, being passionate about the user experience, and the ability to communicate needs and describe requirements, to manage a budget, to guide a development project, and to be comfortable working with a cross-functional, self-organizing team.

The Product Owner at PatientKeeper

Jeff Sutherland, cocreator of Scrum and former CTO of PatientKeeper, Inc., a leading provider of integrated health-care information systems, explains the required qualifications and authority of product owners at the company:

> [A product owner] must be a domain expert, preferably a practicing physician a couple of days a week in one of the leading hospitals in Boston ... an engineering expert, preferably [having] written some apps themselves. ... an expert in user stories, use cases, and software specifications in general and healthcare in particular ... really good with customers and sales people to elicit requirements and recruit physician experts to test-drive prototypes of new functionality ... [and] own the business, the revenue, the customer and sales relationship with respect to features, the physical creation of user stories and any additional specification of the product including all analysis that is related to what the customer wants. [Our product owners] have no help other than developers and other members of the product owner team. The first couple of hires we made couldn't do this. Repeated training, coaching and getting the right person in the job made it happen.[2]

WORKING WITH THE TEAM

As mentioned earlier, the product owner is a member of the Scrum team and relies on collaboration with the ScrumMaster and team. The team itself is self-organizing, cross-functional, and small. It should include all roles required to bring the product to life. All

---

2. From a posting by Jeff Sutherland on the Yahoo! scrumtrainers list on October 2, 2008, and personal communication with Jeff Sutherland on December 16, 2008.

members of the Scrum team must form a close and trusting relationship, a symbiosis, and work together as peers. There must be no
us and them. There can only be *us*.

To allow the Scrum team to flourish, minimize any changes to
it within and across releases. It takes some time for a group of individuals to become a true team—a tightly knit unit with members
who trust and support each other and who work together effectively.
Changing the team's composition makes the team-building process
start all over again, and as a result, productivity and self-organization
suffer. Additionally, establish a long-term partnership between a
Scrum team and its product; every product should be developed by
one or more dedicated teams. This not only facilitates learning, but
it simplifies the allocation of people and resources.

Since the product owner, ScrumMaster, and team need to
closely collaborate on an ongoing basis, it is desirable to colocate *all*
Scrum team members. Take the example of mobile.de. Colocating
the product owners with the ScrumMaster and team increased productivity and morale.[3] If the product owner cannot be permanently
colocated with the team, have as many face-to-face meetings as possible. Remote product owners can benefit from partial colocation,
working on-site with the team for several days in each sprint. For
product owners working on the same site but not yet colocated with
their teams, I often suggest the one-hour rule: Product owners should
spend at least one hour per day with their teams in the team room.

The team room should be conducive to creative and collaborative work. It should be an environment that facilitates communication and interaction, makes work enjoyable, and allows displaying
key artifacts as information radiators (the vision statement, high-priority product backlog items, a software architecture diagram, the
sprint backlog, and the release and sprint burndown). The best team
rooms balance teamwork with the need for privacy and working in
small groups by providing breakout rooms.

---

3. Personal communication with Philip Missler, CTO at mobile.de, on June 22, 2009.

COLLABORATING WITH THE SCRUMMASTER

Just as a sports team requires a coach to play consistently at the highest level, so every Scrum team needs a ScrumMaster.[4] The ScrumMaster supports the product owner and team, protects the team and the process, and intervenes appropriately when required to ensure that the pace of work is sustainable, that the team stays healthy and motivated, and that no technical debt is incurred.[5]

The product owner and ScrumMaster roles complement each other: The product owner is primarily responsible for the "what"—creating the right product. The ScrumMaster is primarily responsible for the "how"—using Scrum the right way. The two aspects are depicted in Figure 1.1. Only when the right product is created with the right process is enduring success achieved.

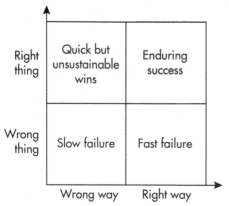

FIGURE 1.1 Doing the right thing the right way

---

4. Professional rugby teams, for instance, have several coaches, including an attack coach, a forwards coach, a defense coach, a scrum coach, a kicking coach, and the head coach.

5. Technical debt and sustainable pace are discussed in detail in Chapter 4 and Chapter 5, respectively.

Since the product owner and ScrumMaster roles are designed to balance each other, playing both roles is overwhelming and unsustainable. One individual should never be both ScrumMaster and product owner.

WORKING WITH CUSTOMERS, USERS, AND OTHER STAKEHOLDERS

The customer, who is the person purchasing the product, and the user, who is the individual using the product, determine the success or failure of the product. Only if enough customers buy the product and the users find it beneficial will the product be a success in the marketplace. Notice that the customer and the user may not be the same person. They may also not have the same needs. Take the example of an electronic spreadsheet. The needs of its users might include ease of use and high productivity. The company purchasing the product, on the other hand, might be concerned about the total cost of ownership and data security.

To create a winning product, the product owner, ScrumMaster, and team must develop an intimate understanding of customer and user needs, and how these needs can best be met. The best way to do this is to involve customers and users early and continuously in the development process. Asking customers to provide feedback on prototypes, inviting customer representatives to sprint review meetings, and releasing software early and frequently are great ways to learn from customers. Teams should bear in mind that the product is only a means to an end—to help the customer and to generate the desired benefits for the company developing it, not an end in itself. As Theodore Levitt famously put it, "People don't want a quarter-inch drill, they want a quarter-inch hole." It is only when we focus on the customer that we develop the best possible solution.

In addition to customers and users, product owners should involve other stakeholders, such as representatives from marketing, sales, and service, early and regularly by asking them to attend the sprint review meetings. The meetings allow the representatives to see the product grow, to interact with the Scrum team, and to share questions, concerns, and ideas. Bryson (2004) provides an overview of helpful techniques to identify and analyze stakeholders.

Product Marketers and Project Managers

Some companies distinguish between strategic and tactical product management aspects and employ separate roles for each, a product marketer and a (technical) product manager. Product marketers tend to be outward-facing; their primary responsibility is to understand the market, manage the product road map, and look after the cumulative profits across releases. Product managers tend to be inward-facing; their responsibilities consist of detailed feature description, prioritization, and collaboration with the development team. In Scrum, the product owner takes on all of these responsibilities. For strategic product management aspects, the product owner may receive support from a portfolio manager, from a vice president, or even from the CEO, depending on the size of the company and the importance of the project. For help with pricing and marketing communications, the product owner may turn to a product marketer and senior salesperson. For the tactical aspects, the product owner can count on the ScrumMaster's and team's support. Uniting the two product management aspects achieves end-to-end authority and accountability. We avoid handoffs, waiting, and delays as well as miscommunication and defects.

You may have noticed that I have not mentioned the role of the project manager on a Scrum team. There is a reason: Project management responsibilities are no longer exercised by one person. They are split across the members of the Scrum team instead. The product owner, for instance, is responsible for managing the release scope and date, managing the budget, communicating progress, and managing the stakeholders. The team takes on the task of identifying, estimating, and managing the tasks. The project manager role is therefore redundant. This does not mean that the individuals working as project managers are no longer needed. The opposite is true. Former project managers often become great ScrumMasters. I have also seen project managers successfully transition into the product owner role.

SCALING THE PRODUCT OWNER ROLE

Before I describe product ownership practices for large Scrum projects, here's a general warning: Avoid large projects. Start small and quickly develop a product with the minimum functionality, as discussed in Chapter 2. If you have to employ a large project, scale slowly and grow the project organically by adding one team at a time. Starting with too many people causes products to be overly complex, making future product updates time-consuming and expensive.[6]

The Chief Product Owner

Large Scrum projects consist of many small teams. Each team needs a product owner, but one product owner can look after only a limited number of teams. How many teams a single product owner can support without being overworked or neglecting some responsibilities depends on a number of factors. These include the product's newness, its complexity, and the domain knowledge of the teams. My experience suggests that a product owner usually cannot look after more than two teams in a sustainable manner. Consequently, when more than two teams are required, several product owners have to collaborate. This seems to create a dilemma: The product owner is one person, but we require several product owners on a large Scrum project. The solution is to put

---

6. This insight is captured in Conway's Law (Conway 1968). It states that the structure of the organization developing a product is likely to influence the architecture of the product. If a project starts with three teams, for instance, chances are that the architecture will consist of three major subsystems.

one person in charge of creating and implementing the product vision. In doing so, we introduce a hierarchy of collaborating product owners with an overall or chief product owner at the top—similar to chefs in a restaurant working together with one cook as the chef de cuisine, the head chef.[7]

The chief product owner guides the other product owners. This individual ensures that needs and requirements are consistently communicated to the various teams, and that the project-wide progress is optimized. This includes facilitating collaborative decision making as well as having the final say if no consensus can be reached. If the project grows organically by starting off with one team, the very first product owner typically becomes the chief product owner.

Product Owner Hierarchies

Product owner hierarchies vary from a small team of product owners with a chief product owner to a complex structure with several levels of collaborating product owners. Let's have a look at the two options, starting with the simpler one.

The project organization depicted in Figure 1.2 consists of three teams and three product owners. Each product owner looks after one team. The product owners form a product owner team with product owner B acting as the chief product owner. Even though there is a chief product owner, the product owner hierarchy is flat. Here is an example of how the project organization can be applied: A client of mine employs a product owner team responsible for a web portal and its applications. Four product owners and a chief product owner collaborate closely. Each product owner looks after an individual application. The chief product owner is in charge of the entire product, comprising all applications and the portal.

---

7. The top-level product owner is not always called *chief product owner*. Schwaber uses the term *overall product owner* (2007); Larman and Vodde call the chief product owner simply *product owner* (2009).

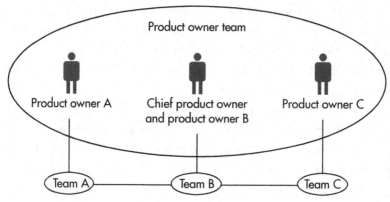

FIGURE 1.2 Simple product owner hierarchy

Figure 1.3 shows another option suitable for larger Scrum projects, which is based on Schwaber (2007, 70–73).

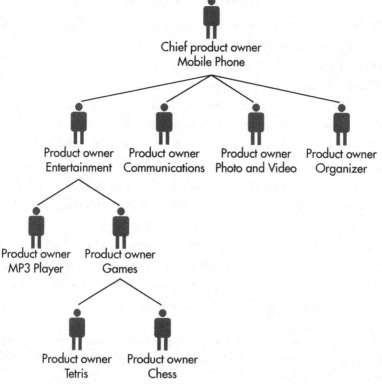

FIGURE 1.3 Complex product owner hierarchy

The project organization partially depicted in Figure 1.3 consists of four layers and nine product owners.[8] Each product owner guides and assists lower-level colleagues. The top-level product owner is the chief product owner in charge of the entire development effort and is responsible for the product's success. The product owners now form a rather extensive hierarchy.

Note that a complex product owner hierarchy introduces a certain specialization of the individual product owner jobs. The chief product owner leads the overall development effort, coordinating with customers and other stakeholders. The lower-level product owners are more focused on their features or subsystems and work closely with the development teams. Schwaber (2007, 72) notes:

> The Product Owner plans, composes, distributes, and tracks work from his or her level down. ... The higher the level is, the harder the Product Owner's ... job is. The responsibility of Product-level jobs usually requires someone with Vice President-level or Director-level title and authority.

Choosing the Right Product Owners

Finding the right person to fill the product owner role is challenging enough when only one product owner is needed. How do we choose the right product owners on large projects? Understanding the different ways we can structure the teams on a large project helps answer the question. There are two ways to organize teams that are creating product increments: as feature teams or as component teams (Pichler 2008, Larman and Vodde 2009). A feature team implements a cohesive set of requirements, such as one or more

---

8. Schwaber (2007, 71) suggests that each product owner forms part of an Integration Scrum Team with the ScrumMaster and team as additional members. Each Integration Scrum Team supports its lower-level teams. In Figure 1.3, the Scrum Integration Team "Games" would support the Scrum teams "Tetris" and "Chess," for instance.

themes or features. The result is an executable vertical slice that cuts across major parts of the software architecture. A component team creates a component or subsystem.

Both team setups are orthogonal: Feature teams are organized around product backlog items, component teams around the software architecture. Both have advantages and disadvantages. Component teams, for instance, ensure architectural integrity and reuse. Unfortunately, they often cannot consume product backlog items expressed as user stories or use cases but instead require detailed technical requirements. In addition, they have to integrate their work results to create a product increment. Both properties create overhead. Feature teams, on the other hand, can usually work in parallel. They encounter fewer integration issues and can consume the requirements stated in the product backlog. Ensuring architectural integrity and reuse can be a challenge, though. As a rule of thumb, organizations should employ feature teams whenever possible and use component teams only if they must.

Since the product owner of a component team has to help translate product backlog items into technical requirements, the best individual to serve in that role is usually an architect or a senior developer rather than a product manager. If a project consists of three feature teams and one component team, for instance, it is likely to require three product managers and one architect to fill the product owner roles—assuming that one of the product owners is the chief product owner.

COMMON MISTAKES

Applying the product owner role means entering new territory for many organizations. And the path to effective product ownership is littered with pitfalls and traps. This section will help you avoid some of the most common mistakes.

The Underpowered Product Owner

A project with an underpowered product owner is much like a car with an underpowered engine: The car runs, but it struggles when the going gets tough. An underpowered product owner lacks empowerment. There may be several causes: The product owner does not have enough management attention; the sponsorship comes from the wrong level or the wrong person; management does not fully trust the product owner or finds it difficult to delegate decision-making authority. As a consequence, the product owner struggles to do an effective job, for instance, to align the Scrum team, stakeholders, and customers or to exclude requirements from the release. A product owner of a new-product development project I worked with, for instance, had to consult his boss, the head of the line of business, for every major decision. Not surprisingly, this caused delays and eroded the team's confidence in the product owner. Ensure that the product owner is fully empowered and receives support and trust from the right person.

The Overworked Product Owner

Being overworked is not just unhealthy and unsustainable on a personal level; overworked product owners quickly become bottlenecks and limit the project's progress. Symptoms of an overworked product owner include neglecting product backlog grooming, missing sprint planning or review meetings, and not being available for questions or giving answers only after a long delay. Overworked product owners are at odds with the Agile Manifesto's concept of sustainable pace. "Agile processes promote sustainable development. The sponsors, developers, and users should be able to maintain a constant pace indefinitely" (Beck et al. 2001).

There are two main causes of product owner overburden: not enough time to perform the role and not enough support from the team. Availability tends to be an issue when the product owner role is just one of many jobs competing for time and attention or when the product owner looks after too many products or teams. Not enough support from the team is rooted in a wrong understanding of product ownership: Even though there is one product owner, most of the product owner work is carried out collaboratively. The team and ScrumMaster must support the product owner.

To avoid an overworked product owner, try the following: First, free the individual from all other responsibilities. Start with the assumption that being a product owner is a full-time job, and that one product owner can look after only one product and one team. Second, ensure that the team makes time in every sprint to collaborate with the product owner. Scrum allocates up to 10% of the team's capacity in every sprint for supporting the product owner (Schwaber 2007). Not only does collaboration spread the work across many shoulders; it also leverages the team's collective knowledge and creativity.

The Partial Product Owner

Some organizations split the product owner role and distribute its duties across several people, for instance, by employing a product manager and a "product owner." The product manager takes care of the product marketing and product management aspects, owns the vision, is outward-facing, and keeps in touch with the market. The "product owner" is inward-facing, drives the sprints, and works with the team. In these cases, the so-called product owner is little more than a product backlog item writer. This approach reinforces old barriers, blurs responsibility and authority, and causes handoffs, delays, and other waste.

Instead of splitting the product owner role, organizations should face the challenge of applying the role properly. One person should be in charge of the strategic and the tactical product management aspects. This may well require organizational changes, including adapting job roles and career paths and developing individuals to take on a rich set of responsibilities, as discussed in Chapter 6.

The Distant Product Owner

A distant product owner works separately from the team. Distance may evoke images of a globalized world with the product owner on one continent and the team on another. But distance comes in many forms and degrees. It starts with working on the same site in different rooms, and it ends with product owner and team being separated across continents and time zones (Simons 2004). I have found recurring issues with distant product owners, including mistrust, miscommunication, misalignment, and slow progress. There is a reason: "The most efficient and effective method of conveying information to and within a development team is face-to-face conversation" (Beck et al. 2001).

Avoid distant product owners by colocating all Scrum team members. As mentioned earlier, mobile.de experienced a significant productivity and morale increase after colocating its product owner, ScrumMaster, and team. If colocation is not an option, the product owner should spend as much time as possible in the same room as the rest of the Scrum team. Remote product owners should be on-site at least for the sprint planning, the review, and the retrospective meetings. Moving from a distant to a colocated product owner often takes time. It may require hiring and training a local product owner. In some cases, it may also require rethinking the company's product strategy, including where the company develops its products.

The Proxy Product Owner

A proxy product owner is a person acting as a placeholder for the actual product owner. I have found proxy product owners used to compensate for overworked, partial, and distant product owners. At a client of mine, the vice president of product management was asked to take on the product owner role for a business-critical product. Even though he was ideally suited for the job, he struggled to spend enough time with the team. The business analyst on the team consequently stood in as a proxy product owner when the real product owner could not be there. The proxy did most of the product owner work without being empowered. The actual product owner ultimately decided about product backlog prioritization, release planning, and whether to accept or reject work results. What followed was an increase in conflicts and miscommunication, a slowdown in decision making, and a decrease in productivity and morale.

Using a proxy product owner is an attempt to superficially treat a systemic issue. Rather than employing a quick fix, organizations should address the underlying issues. This might require freeing up the product owner from other obligations; colocating the product owner, ScrumMaster, and team; or even finding a new product owner.

The Product Owner Committee

A product owner committee is a group of product owners without anyone in charge of the overall product. There is no one person guiding the group, helping to create a common goal, and facilitating decision making. A product owner committee is in danger of getting caught in endless meetings with conflicting interests and politics—something also referred to as "death by committee." No real progress is achieved; people stop collaborating and start fighting each other. Always ensure that there is one person in charge of the product, an overall or chief product owner who guides the other product owners and facilitates decision making, including product backlog prioritization and release planning.

REFLECTION

The product owner role is a cornerstone of successfully applying agile product management in Scrum. The days of the lonesome product manager locked away in her room and racking her brain to come up with perfect requirements are over. The product owner is a member of the Scrum team and as such is committed to close and ongoing collaboration. The following questions can help you apply the product owner role successfully:

Who represents customers and users at your company?

Who identifies and describes customer needs and product functionality?

Who leads the visioning activities, and who leads the activities that bring the vision to life?

What roles do teamwork and collaborative decision making play?

What would it take to implement the product owner role, as described in this chapter?

2

. . .

ENVISIONING THE PRODUCT

It wasn't fun to have a telephone conference in the early 1990s. Participants would often have to turn their heads away from the table and shout into a microphone. When people talked simultaneously, their voices cut out, turning conversation into gibberish. Polycom, a company that specializes in telepresence, video, voice, and content-sharing solutions, recognized that its customers needed telephone conferences that felt more like natural face-to-face conversations—without any distortion, echoes, or other interruptions. So Polycom envisioned a product with the following attributes (Lynn and Reilly 2002, 63):

- Superb audio quality—allowing more than one person at a time to speak and still be understood
- Simple to use—no confusing buttons and cords
- First-class looks—belongs in an executive conference room

The resulting product was called SoundStation, which launched in 1992. Its vision was an important stepping-stone toward the product's overwhelming success. This chapter discusses techniques for envisioning a product. We'll start with the content and the qualities of an effective product vision.

THE PRODUCT VISION

"Would you tell me, please, which way I ought to go from here?" Alice asks the Cheshire Cat in Lewis Carroll's novel *Alice's Adventures in Wonderland*. "That depends a good deal on where you want to get to," said the Cat. "I don't much care where –," said Alice. "Then it doesn't matter which way you go," said the Cat (Carroll 1998, 56).

Being able to envision what a new product or the next product version should look like and do is essential for getting there. Envisioning the product results in the product vision—a sketch of the future product.[1] The vision acts the overarching goal, galvanizing and guiding people, and is the product's reason for being. As in the Polycom example, the vision selectively describes the product at a coarse-grained level, capturing the product's essence—the information considered critical to develop and launch a winning product. Demoing product increments to customers and users in the sprint review meetings and releasing software early and frequently validates and refines the vision. An effective vision should answer the following questions:

- Who is going to buy the product? Who is the target customer? Who is going to use the product? Who are its target users?
- Which needs will the product address? What value does the product add?
- Which product attributes are critical for meeting the needs selected and therefore for the success of the product? What will the product roughly look like and do? In which areas is the product going to excel?

---

1. Even though the product vision is not part of the Scrum framework, it is mentioned by Schwaber and Beedle (2002, 34). Ken Schwaber also writes about the vision in *Agile Project Management with Scrum*: "The vision describes why the project is being undertaken and what the desired end state is" (2004, 68).

- How does the product compare against existing products, from both competitors and the same company? What are the product's unique selling points? What is its target price?
- How will the company make money from selling the product? What are the sources of revenue and what is the business model?
- Is the product feasible? Can the company develop and sell the product?

If you plan to use a new product as a springboard for changing your business model, this information should be reflected in the product vision. Take Apple's iPod and iTunes as an example. Apple came to dominate the digital music market by creating a good product, the iPod, and wrapping it in a great business model. The tight integration of iPod and iTunes, the company's online music store, not only provided a convenient way to purchase music online, but it locked in customers. This allowed Apple to change the rules of the game—selling online music at comparatively cheap prices. The company makes small margins on the music but large ones on the MP3 players. An iPod vision would most certainly contain the requirement of seamless integration with iTunes, and the iTunes vision would refer to the business model and the additional revenue made from selling iPods.

DESIRABLE QUALITIES OF THE VISION

The vision should communicate the essence of the future product in a concise manner and describe a shared goal that provides direction but is broad enough to facilitate creativity.

Shared and Unifying

Everyone involved in the development effort should buy into the vision: Scrum team, management, customers, users, and other stakeholders. As Peter Senge puts it: "A vision is truly shared when you and I have a similar picture and are committed to one another having it, not just to each of us, individually, having it" (2006, 192). A shared vision creates alignment and galvanizes everyone involved in the development effort. It facilitates effective teamwork and enables team learning. "When people truly share a vision, they are connected, bound together by a common aspiration" (Senge 2006, 192). If team members have private visions, the individuals end up pulling in different directions rather than toward the common goal. A great way to create a shared vision is to involve the Scrum team and stakeholders in the visioning activities.

Broad and Engaging

The product vision should describe a broad and engaging goal: a goal that guides the development efforts but leaves enough room for creativity, a goal that engages and inspires people. Marissa Mayer, vice president of search product and user experience at Google, describes how Google leverages the vision:

> We bring together a team of people who are really passion-ate about [a] subject. I think it's interesting: We still don't do very high-definition product specs. If you write a 70-page document that says this is the product you're sup-posed to build, you actually push the creativity out with [the] process. The engineer who says, you know what, there's a feature here that you forgot that I would really like to add. You don't want to push that creativity out of the product. The consensus-driven approach where the team works together to build a vision around what they're building and still leaves enough room for each member of the team to participate creatively, is really inspiring and yields us some of the best outcomes we've had.[2]

---

2. "Inside Google's New-Product Process," BusinessWeek.com, June 30, 2006, www.businessweek.com/technology/content/jun2006/tc20060629_411177.htm.

Resist the temptation to provide too much detail or to over-specify the product. More functionality is discovered and captured in the product backlog as the project progresses.

Short and Sweet

When it comes to the product vision, less is more. The vision should be brief and concise. It should contain only information critical to the success of the product. The blockbuster products in Lynn and Reilly's ten-year study have no more than six product attributes, for instance (2002). The product vision is not, therefore, a feature list, nor should it provide unnecessary detail. Agile project management expert Jim Highsmith explains, "Coming up with fifteen or twenty product capabilities or features proves to be easy. Selecting the three or four that would incent someone to buy the product is difficult" (2009, 97). Product development expert Donald Reinertsen agrees: "Most successful products have a clear and simple value proposition. Buyers typically make their choice between competing products on the basis of three or four key factors" (1997, 174–75).

The product vision is usually concise if it passes Moore's elevator test. "Can you explain your product in the time it takes to ride up in an elevator?" (2006, 152). If the answer is no, the vision is likely to be too long or complex.

THE MINIMAL MARKETABLE PRODUCT

To create a vision, the Scrum team has to peek into the future and state what it *believes* the future product will roughly look like and do. For anyone not blessed with perfect foresight, predicting the future correctly is notoriously difficult. After all, the only thing certain about the future is that it is uncertain. No market research technique can deliver forecasts that are 100% accurate. And making a completely fail-safe investment is an illusion. Cooper, for instance, states a failure rate of 25% to 45% for new products (2001, 10); some studies reveal even higher odds of failure. Markets develop unexpectedly and customer reaction is hard to predict, as the following story illustrates.[3]

When Expertcity released an interactive technical support system in 1999, the company had high hopes. The market research data indicated that the new product would be a big success. Unfortunately, the product did not deliver what the company had hoped for. Expertcity noticed, though, that users had started employing one part of the product, a desktop-sharing utility, in a novel, unanticipated way. Customers were using the feature to administer computers in a remote location. The company took the right action and quickly adapted the product, turning it into a tool for remote administration. The modified product was called GoToMyPC. It was so successful that Citrix decided to acquire Expertcity for $225 million in 2003. GoToMyPC now forms part of the Citrix Online suite. Expertcity's original product vision may have been wrong, but its ability to adapt enabled the company to turn certain failure into unmitigated success.

As our ability to predict the future is limited, our best chance of success is to envision the *minimal marketable* product, a product with minimum functionality that meets the selected customer needs.[4] Take the iPhone, which launched in 2007. The phone's unrivaled user experience made its competitors blush; it set a new

---

3. The accuracy of predicting a market response is influenced by the market dynamics and the degree of innovation of the product. For steady-state markets and products exhibiting continuous or incremental innovation, it may be possible to anticipate the market response fairly well. For other markets and products it is difficult or even impossible—as in the case of disruptive innovation. Christensen (1997, 143) observes: "Markets that do not exist cannot be analyzed."

4. The term *minimal marketable product* is a reference to Mark Denne and Jane Cleland-Huang's work. In their book *Software by Numbers* (2004) they coin the term *minimal marketable feature set* to denote the smallest amount of functionality creating value for a customer. The idea of delivering a small set of features quickly and enhancing the product incrementally dates back to Tom Gilb's evolutionary delivery method (Gilb 1988).

standard for smartphones. One of the secrets behind its success is the narrow set of customer needs Apple selected. The company avoided the trap of trying to please too many people at once, of trying to copy all the features competitors offered. Instead, Apple took a fresh look at what smartphones should look like and do and deliberately left out some functionality. The original iPhone shipped without many features that were standard on existing phones: copy and paste, the ability to send text messages to multiple recipients, and a software development kit, for instance. These limitations, though, did not hinder its success. Paring down the functionality allowed Apple to develop and ship the product within a competitive time frame and gave the company a significant lead over its competitors. Building on the success of the first iPhone version, Apple launched the 3G model in 2008, extending the capabilities of the phone in terms of both hardware and software. It also entered a new market segment by targeting business users.

Contrast the iPhone success story with another Apple product: the Apple Newton, first launched in 1993 after five years of development. Remember those Apple ads that promised a PDA that could do all sorts of wonderful things, including recognizing your handwriting? When it was finally shipped, the Newton proved to be too bulky and heavy. Worse, its most important feature, the handwriting recognition, did not work properly. The product underperformed and was finally withdrawn from the market in 1998. In hindsight, Apple was overly ambitious with its Newton plans. The company launched a product that tried to do too much at once and failed.

Creating a minimal product provides us with a number of advantages, as noted by Smith and Reinertsen (1997) and Denne and Cleland-Huang (2004).[5] The product is launched more quickly and time to market is reduced; functionality is released in a more timely manner. The product is developed at a lower cost and generates a

---

5. Smith and Reinertsen (1997) call the technique of breaking innovation into smaller, faster steps *incremental innovation*.

higher return on investment. Payments are received earlier, improv-
ing the cash flow, and learning is accelerated. By reducing time to
market, we are able to listen and respond to the marketplace more frequently, rather than trying to outguess it. Getting a minimal product
out quickly also improves risk mitigation. Less money is lost if the
product underperforms and has to be withdrawn from the market
early. This allows us to build the possibility of failure into our strategy,
an approach Google has embraced. Marissa Mayer of Google
explains: "We anticipate that we're going to throw out a lot of products, but [people] will remember the ones that really matter and the
ones that have a lot of user potential."[6]

As the future is uncertain, the vision should cover the next
product version. Even if Steve Jobs's long-term dream was to dominate the mobile phone market, it was certainly not the goal for the
first iPhone. Grand ambitions are best realized one step at a time.
"There is only one move that really counts: the next one" (Gilb
1988, 97). Once the vision is available, it is turned into a shippable
product by leveraging customer and user feedback; the feedback is
collected by demoing product increments in the sprint review meetings and by releasing software early and frequently. Working this
way allows the Scrum team to find out quickly if the right product is
being developed. If not, the vision is ill conceived and has to be
adapted.

Note that the vision may be implemented by more than one
release. Take the example of the first version of Google Chrome.
Many nonpublic releases of the browser and a public beta in
September 2008 preceded the launch of version 1.0 in December
2008. A longer-term outlook on a product's growth can be captured
in the form of a product road map, as I discuss later in this chapter.

---

6. "So Much Fanfare, So Few Hits," BusinessWeek.com, July 10, 2006, www.busi-
nessweek.com/magazine/content/06_28/b3992051.htm. A similar attitude is por-
trayed by the motto "You have to kiss a lot of frogs to find a prince," as Art Fry of 3M
famously observed. Note that a handsome prince pays for many frogs.

SIMPLICITY

Simplicity facilitates creating a product with the minimum functionality that is easy to use. Don't mistake simplicity for creating simplistic products. As Leonardo da Vinci said, "Simplicity is the ultimate sophistication."

Ockham's Razor

Using simplicity as a guiding principle follows a long-standing tradition. In the fourteenth century, Franciscan friar William of Ockham allegedly postulated that given a choice between functionally equivalent designs, the simplest design should be selected (Lidwell, Holden, and Butler 2003, 142). This insight is known as Ockham's razor.

Simplicity is not only about the aesthetics of a product. It means focusing on the product's essence, building only what is really needed, and being able to adjust and extend the product easily. A simple yet adequate product is easy to use—think of Apple's iPod. The click-wheel-based iPod with its buttons on the wheel is simple and minimalist but offers all essential functions. As Beck and Andres put it: "Projects that move towards simplicity improve both the humanity and productivity of their software development" (2005, 110).

Less Is More

Common sense seems to suggest that beating the competition requires a superior product with more functionality. We tend to equate having more features with being better and more desirable. Not so, says 37Signals (2006), a company that provides award-winning, easy-to-use web-based applications. The company designs its products with simplicity in mind and focuses on the product essentials.

> *Do less than your competitors to beat them ... Take what-*
> *ever you think your product should be and cut it in half*
> *... Start off with a lean, smart app and let it gain trac-*
> *tion. Then you can start to add to the solid foundation*
> *you've built.*

Simplicity expert and MIT professor John Maeda agrees: "The simplest way to achieve simplicity is through thoughtful reduction. When in doubt, just remove" (2006, 1). And Steve Jobs is quoted as saying, "Innovation is not about saying yes to everything. It's about saying no to all but the most crucial features." The Manifesto for Agile Software Development shares this insight, recognizing simplicity as one of its 12 principles and calling it "the art of maximizing the amount of work not done" (Beck et al. 2001). Whenever you have an idea for a new feature or you discover a new requirement, ask yourself if the new functionality is critical to the success of the product. If not, discard the idea. This results in a product that is simple and uncluttered, that offers only the features a customer or user needs.

Simple User Interfaces

A company that explicitly embraces simplicity as a central user experience principle is Google. "Google doesn't set out to create feature-rich products; our best designs include only the features that people need to accomplish their goals. Ideally, even products that require large feature sets and complex visual designs appear to be simple as well as powerful. ... Our hope is to evolve products in new directions instead of just adding more features."[7] Designing simple user interfaces has paid off for Google, according to Lidwell, Holden, and Butler: "While other Internet search services were racing to add advertising services and ad hoc functions to their Web sites, Google kept its design simple and efficient. The result is the best performing and easiest to use search service on the Web" (2003, 143). And

---

7. "Ten principles that contribute to a Googley user experience," www.google.com /corporate/ux.html.

Bernard Girard, author of *The Google Way* (2009, 34), argues that simplicity has helped AdWords, Google's advertising program, to be so successful:

> *Like the intuitive Macintosh GUI that makes Apple prod-ucts so friendly and easy to use, the design and user-friend-liness of Google's AdWords interface has helped make it a winner. Any advertiser can easily understand how to place an ad....*

CUSTOMER NEEDS AND PRODUCT ATTRIBUTES

Customer needs and product attributes are at the heart of the vision and deserve close attention. Selecting the relevant customer needs tells us which market or market segment we are going to address. By focusing on the needs, we view the product as a means to an end — serving the customer or user. Product attributes, on the other hand, are the critical properties the product must have in order to meet these needs. A touch screen, for instance, is a product attribute. The underlying need for that attribute is likely to be ease of use. Attributes can be of a functional or nonfunctional nature. Functional proper-ties are specific product functions or features, such as being able to make or receive calls. Nonfunctional attributes include perfor-mance, robustness, style, design, and usability. Nonfunctional attrib-utes can be an important differentiator — they can impact the user experience as well as the extensibility and maintainability of the product, which in turn influence the total cost of ownership and the product's life expectancy.

Attributes guide the team by constraining the solution space — the set of all possible solutions. By stating customer needs and detailing a minimum set of product attributes, we connect needs to the technical solution, placing the customer at the center of our development effort. Separating needs and attributes allows us to investigate both why the product is required and also what the product should look like and do. It makes it possible to explore different attributes to find out which one is best suited. A touch screen, for example, is one way to provide ease of use. Other, possibly cheaper, alternatives are a small number of large buttons or voice control.

Once we have identified the product attributes, it's often useful to prioritize them; attributes serving several needs are important and should be high priority. Prioritization is particularly helpful when attributes conflict. Consider the following two attributes: interoperability and serviceability. The ability to interoperate with different systems and devices usually requires a certain level of architectural complexity. Serviceability, on the other hand, suggests employing a simple and extensible architecture. The result is tension—the product owner, ScrumMaster, and team have to creatively reconcile the irreconcilable and find the best possible solution to satisfy the customer needs. Cockburn (2005, 147) suggests using the following prioritization factors for product attributes:

- Sacrifice others for this
- Try to keep
- Sacrifice these for others

To prioritize serviceability over interoperability, for example, we would *sacrifice other* attributes *for* serviceability. At the same time, we would *try to keep* interoperability.

A useful, simple, and cost-effective tool for capturing needs and attributes is a set of paper cards. Cards support teamwork and can be easily annotated and amended. We can group them, put them up on the wall, and move them around. Once the visioning work is done, we can glue the cards on flip-chart paper, hang them up in the team room, and put a copy on the project's wiki.

THE BIRTH OF THE VISION

The early days of every product are surrounded by myths and legends; there is no perfect formula to conceive ideas and evolve them into a vision. This section discusses two approaches to developing the vision for a new product: pet projects and Scrum. Whatever you do, keep the visioning work to a minimum and quickly release a first product increment, or demo it to customers and users. Listen to the responses to see if you are shooting for the right goal. Then adapt. And refrain from putting too many controls and procedures around the visioning work. Otherwise, innovation and creativity are strangled; employees spend their time filling out forms rather than innovating.

Using Pet Projects

At companies like Google, developers are encouraged to spend 20% of their time on "pet projects." These private research projects result in new ideas implemented as prototypes. The results justify Google's investment: Half of all products released by Google in the last six months of 2005 started as pet projects (Mayer 2006). The developers who came up with the original idea continue to work on the project that brings the product to life, as in the case of Google's Chrome browser. Ben Goodger and Darin Fisher, two of the engineers who came up with the original prototype, played an important role on the Chrome development project (Levy 2008).[8] Ken Schwaber (2007, 80) favors this approach to developing new ideas:

> I recommend you set aside a part of every employee's time to pursue activities that are outside their current Scrum teams and that benefit the enterprise. I recommend an allowance of 20 percent of their time. Let people coalesce

---

8. The Google browser project was led by product manager Brian Rakowski (Levy 2008).

into interest groups where they work together. Some of this
can be spent working with peers in sustaining and enhanc-
ing functional expertise. Some of the work can be research-
ing and prototyping new ideas. The yellow sticky notes of
3M and Gmail at Google were developed in this way.

Using Scrum

If a larger effort is necessary to create the vision, use Scrum to do the job. Ask the product owner, ScrumMaster, and team to carry out the visioning activities, with the product owner leading the effort. At first, the product backlog will contain visioning deliverables, such as "Prototypes exploring user interface design options are available" and "Customer interviews are carried out." As the work progresses, the product backlog will include the high-level attributes that describe the future product, according to the product vision. Each visioning sprint will create an increment that forms a step toward the product vision and ultimately a shippable product. (If only one visioning sprint is required, its output is the product vision.) Take the example of Supermassive Games, a games development studio based in the UK. The company uses visioning sprints to manage the early development work, also called "preproduction." The team creates sketches and prototypes to iterate toward a computer game's vision. The prototypes range from Lego models and concept artwork to software.[9]

The Scrum team that performs the visioning should also carry out the development work, with a few notable exceptions. In some cases, the team may want to include specialists, such as a user experience designer or a service representative, as part of the team for the visioning sprints. Once the vision is available, the specialist might move off the team and become a stakeholder.

---

9. Personal communication with Harvey Wheaton, studio director at Supermassive Games, on October 21, 2009, and November 2, 2009.

TECHNIQUES FOR CREATING THE VISION

This section offers an overview of techniques that are helpful in creating the product vision. It is not intended to be comprehensive, nor does it attempt to describe the techniques in depth. Instead, this section aims to equip you with enough information so you can judge whether the techniques are applicable to your project. These include prototypes and mock-ups; personas and scenarios; use cases and user stories; sequences and storyboards; vision boxes and reviews; and the Kano Model.

Prototypes and Mock-ups

At the start of a new project, we often do not know what we don't know. Worse, our target customers and lead users sometimes don't know what they don't know; they are not in a position to tell us correctly up front what the product must look like and do. Creating the vision is therefore best understood as a discovery process, a process of knowledge acquisition and learning that requires experimentation. Experimentation examines the relationship between cause and effect, manipulating the cause until the desired effect has been achieved. It is as much about cultivating an open, inquisitive, and playful mind as it is about following a stringent process. The key to effective experimentation is to generate the necessary knowledge rapidly by implementing and testing prototypes and mock-ups. These act as vehicles of knowledge creation and learning. They help us understand what the product should roughly look like and do, what technology and architecture options are viable, and if the idea is actually feasible. Prototypes are usually throwaway artifacts that can be created quickly and inexpensively; paper prototypes and sketches are sometimes sufficient to test an idea. Executable prototypes exploring a specific issue are also called *spikes*.

A telecommunications project I worked with, for example, had to fulfill ambitious usability requirements. Market research had shown that the company's products were perceived as less user-friendly than the competition's. So the team built a prototype, consisting of a device mock-up and a throwaway Flash implementation of critical user interface parts. Customers were invited to test the prototype, and their feedback was incorporated in the product design. The end result was a new product with a superior user experience.

Plan, Do, Check, and Act

Organized experimentation follows a four-step process also known as the Deming cycle. We first develop a hypothesis (plan). We then validate the hypothesis (do) and review the results (check). If the experiment was unsuccessful, we adapt the hypothesis (if required) and carry out another round of experimentation, either to refine the result or to try out a different approach (act). Thomas Edison, the creator of the first commercially successful electric light bulb, knew about the necessity of trial and error, the need to fail in order to bring new products to life. As he famously said,

> If I find 10,000 ways something won't work, I haven't failed. I am not discouraged, because every wrong attempt discarded is another step forward.

Personas and Scenarios

Personas help us select our target customers. Scenarios allow us to understand how the product changes their lives (Cooper 1999). A persona is a "hypothetical archetype" representing a target customer or user. You can think of a persona as a specific instance of a use case actor or a user role. Personas have names. Their descriptions include information relevant to their use of the product: for instance, their job roles, skills, or interests.

Once we have found the right personas, we can investigate how the product we are about to develop will influence their lives. To do this, we create scenarios that describe how the persona achieves a goal without and with the product. A formal way to create these scenarios is to create two consumption maps: one of the activities necessary to realize a particular goal without the product, the other of the activities that would be required in a future state, with the product in use (Womack and Jones 2005). Using scenarios and consumption maps allows us to establish the value proposition of the product: Are the selected attributes necessary? Do they provide a benefit for all personas? Can we identify more critical product attributes?

Vision Box and Trade Journal Review

Two effective techniques for determining the product's value-added and selling points are a product's vision box and a trade journal review. A vision box is a mock-up of the package in which the product might ship. To build a vision box, the Scrum team selects a product name, a graphical representation of the product, and three bullet points that would sell the product; the information is then placed on the front of the box. More details can be added on the back (Highsmith 2009, 96–97). To write the trade journal review, the Scrum team members explore what they would like to read about the product once it is launched (Cohn 2009, 232). The exercise is quick and easy to apply. It can also be used to test if there is a commonly understood and shared vision.

Kano Model

The Kano Model helps us select the right functionality to create an attractive product (Kano 1984). It tells us how satisfied the customer is likely to be when we implement a certain product attribute. The model distinguishes between three types of functions: basics, performance functions, and delighters. Let's use a mobile phone to understand how the Kano Model works. *Basic functions* of a mobile phone include switching the phone on and off; making and receiving calls; and composing, sending, receiving, and reading text messages. These rudimentary functions are necessary to sell a product but quickly cause customer satisfaction to stagnate. For instance, adding another button to switch the phone on and off would not add any value. Failing to provide a basic function usually renders the product useless. *Performance functions* lead to a linear increase in satisfaction. They follow the principle "The more, the better." For instance, the lighter the phone is and the more quickly it starts up, the more satisfied customers tend to be with it. Customers cannot get enough of performance requirements. They are not sufficient, though, to differentiate the product in the marketplace. *Delighters*, as the name suggests, delight and excite customers. An attractive product design and the ability to personalize the phone are examples of delighters. Delighters can be related to latent and hidden customer needs—needs customers were not aware of. They are those product functions that provide a competitive advantage and a unique selling proposition.

The challenge is to bundle basic, performance, and delighter attributes in such a way that the desired benefits are maximized. Note that it is often useful to apply the Kano Model to the product vision and the product backlog. Like the SoundStation vision that began this chapter, visions usually focus on performance attributes and delighters and are unlikely to state any basics. These can be found in the product backlog. Note that the Kano Model makes an interesting prediction: Over time, delighters will eventually become performance functions and performers will become basics. Eventually, products lose their competitive advantages as the competition begins to provide similar products. To stay ahead, companies have to regularly update the product and deliver new delighters. This correlation is another reason to quickly launch an initial product and to grow it using regular updates.

VISIONING AND THE PRODUCT ROAD MAP

So far, this chapter has focused on envisioning a new product, which is particularly challenging. As the product matures and incremental updates are released, the visioning effort usually declines. But the new product versions still need goals. A product road map allows the Scrum team to capture the goals of upcoming product versions; visioning now forms a part of creating and updating the product road map.

A product road map is a planning artifact that shows how the product is likely to evolve across product versions, facilitating a dialogue between the Scrum team and the stakeholders. A road map allows organizations to coordinate the development and launch of related products, for instance, a product line or a product portfolio. I recommend keeping product road maps simple and focused on the essentials. A product road map should state for each version the projected launch date, the target customers and their needs, and the top three to five features. Don't worry about the details. These will emerge and be captured in the product backlog. Be aware that a product road map can never replace carefully inspecting the market response and adapting the product accordingly. It simply states how we *believe* the product is likely to evolve based on our current understanding of the market. Product road maps are living documents; they evolve and change.

Create a product road map once the product has been successfully introduced into the marketplace. (Crafting a five-year product road map before any release is deployed provides little benefit; it paints a dream rather than anticipating reality.) When you create a product road map, involve all the relevant people. This will include the Scrum team and might also involve the person in charge of the product portfolio, representatives from other product development teams, and stakeholders. Make sure your product road map covers a realistic planning horizon. Depending on the market and the product's lifecycle stage, focus on the next 6 to 12 months rather than predicting the next two to three years.

MINIMAL PRODUCTS AND PRODUCT VARIANTS

As a product matures, it might address a growing number of customer needs, for instance, by serving customers in different segments and different regions. Dealing with many diverse needs makes it more difficult to create product updates with minimum functionality; more and more features are required to support an ever-growing number of customers and users. To solve the problem, we take advantage of product variants. Each variant addresses a specific customer group and market segment. Take Microsoft's popular diagramming program Visio, for instance. The 2007 edition is available in two variants: Office Visio Standard 2007 and Office Visio Professional 2007. Whereas the former acts as an "essential visualization tool," the professional version extends Visio Standard 2007 "to help IT and business users visualize, analyze, and communicate complex information, systems, and processes."[10] The two variants serve different market segments: home users and enterprise users with limited diagramming needs, and professional users in need of advanced diagramming functionality.

While product variants can be powerful allies, be aware that too many variants lead to a bloated product portfolio, high support cost, and overwhelmed consumers. Imagine if Microsoft offered four Office Visio 2007 versions: Essentials, Standard, Professional, and Deluxe. Consumers would be confused by too many choices and find it difficult to make a purchase decision.[11]

---

10. See http://office.microsoft.com.

11. Note that Microsoft used to offer three Visio editions, Standard, Pro, and Tech, in the late 1990s. Since then the company has streamlined its portfolio.

There is another potential drawback: Product variants carry the danger of implementing functionality over and over again, causing high development and maintenance costs. Creating a set of assets shared by the variants addresses this issue. These assets are also called a platform. Apple's iPhone and iPod Touch employ common components, for instance. As you recognize the need for commonality, don't fall into the trap of aspiring to build the perfect mega platform. Start small. Grow the platform organically as the need for product variants arises, and carefully guard the platform's functionality. This approach is likely to result in architecture refactoring, but it mitigates the danger of overengineering the platform.

COMMON MISTAKES

Creating a product vision is a crucial step in taking a product to launch. Watch out for these common visioning mistakes: no vision, prophecy vision, analysis paralysis, we know best what is good for our customers, and big is beautiful.

No Vision

An obvious but surprisingly common mistake is to start product development without a product vision. This happens most often when customers request individual features that are incorporated into the product with no consideration of the connection between them. The result is a product known as *feature soup* (DeMarco et al. 2008, 143–45). Avoid this antipattern by ensuring that a vision is available that clearly states the customer, the selected customer needs, and the critical attributes. This vision will then help determine which features should be implemented and will ensure that a useful and valuable product is created.

Prophecy Vision

Even though the vision paints a picture of the future product, the envisioned future might never come true. Progressing the vision into a product is an entrepreneurial act that carries the risk of failure. Remember how Expertcity's product vision resulted in a product that did not live up to expectations? Even with a vision, failure can and does happen. As in the case of Expertcity, though, failure can be a stepping-stone to success. After all, GoToMyPC was born out of an unsuccessful first release. To minimize any potential loss or damage from an inaccurate forecast, select a narrow set of customer needs and quickly release a product increment. Then inspect and adapt.

Analysis Paralysis

As mentioned earlier, don't overdo the up-front market research work and avoid getting caught in the analysis-paralysis trap—carrying out more and more research work without making any real progress. Overdoing market research not only wastes time and money, it also carries the danger of never delivering an attractive product in a timely manner. Understanding the market and caring for customers are important; being purely customer-driven and not having your own strong vision of what the product should look like and do are unlikely to deliver success.

A common cause of analysis paralysis is being overly concerned with making fail-safe investments. Companies exhibiting this mind-set are often not tolerant of failure and have a "get it right the first time" attitude. Management demands accurate forecasts of the future product's performance, including a precise quantification of market share and profits, before a vision is approved. Analysis paralysis is prevented by keeping the visioning work to a minimum, getting the product out as fast as possible, and swiftly adapting it to the actual market response.

We Know Best What Is Good for Our Customers

Some companies gravitate toward the other extreme and close themselves off from the market. They rely solely on management's intuition or the technical brilliance of their developers. These companies believe they know best what's good for their customers. The big risk, of course, is that the company invests time and money in developing a product that nobody wants. The best way to prevent innovating in an ivory tower is to incorporate customers and users into the development process by inviting them to sprint review meetings and by releasing software early and frequently.

Big Is Beautiful

Creating products that launch with an abundance of functionality can make great news stories, as Preston Smith and Donald Reinertsen note (1998, 67):

> We are all drawn to tales of heroic success in product development. A development team steps up to the challenge of a seemingly impossible project and puts in super-human efforts. ... These projects are like the long touchdown passes that drive the fans wild. They are much more exciting than the running game that rolls down the field 10 yards at a time.

Exciting as they may be, big-bang development efforts have a dark side: They consume lots of time and money, and they exhibit a high risk of failure. "Companies frequently make the mistake of trying to pursue a perfect solution that gets everything right from day one. The results are often over-engineered, expensive products that don't actually work very well" (Anthony et al. 2008, 125). A big-bang effort also makes it very difficult to evolve the product based on customer and user feedback, as so much functionality is predetermined.

Avoid this mistake by starting with a product that addresses a narrow set of customer needs and provides the minimum functionality required. Release early and frequently to incorporate customer and user feedback. Launch the product quickly, inspect the market response, and adapt the product accordingly.

REFLECTION

Make sure the Scrum team has a shared vision of the future product. Keep the vision humble and focused on the upcoming product version. Think big, but start small. Put the vision to the test by inviting customers and users to sprint review meetings and by quickly releasing a product increment. Then evolve your product based on their feedback. The following questions will help you apply the vision concepts discussed:

> *Do your products follow shared goals?*
>
> *How are the goals derived and who creates them?*
>
> *What would it take to create a vision with the qualities described in this chapter?*
>
> *How would such a vision improve your innovation process?*

3
• • •

WORKING WITH THE PRODUCT
BACKLOG

Few artifacts in Scrum are as popular as the product backlog. And there is a reason: The product backlog is beautifully simple—a prioritized list of the outstanding work necessary to bring the product to life. Its items can include the exploration of customer needs or various technical options, a description of both functional and nonfunctional requirements, the work necessary to launch the product, and other items as well, such as setting up the environment or remediating defects. The product backlog supersedes traditional requirements artifacts, such as market and product requirements specifications. The product owner is responsible for managing the product backlog; the ScrumMaster, team, and stakeholders contribute to it. Together, they discover the product's functionality.

This chapter discusses the product backlog along with techniques for effectively grooming it. In addition, we look at some of the more complicated product backlog applications, including how to handle nonfunctional requirements and how to scale a product backlog for large projects.

THE DEEP QUALITIES OF THE PRODUCT BACKLOG

The product backlog has four qualities: It is detailed appropriately, estimated, emergent, and prioritized, making it DEEP.[1] Let's look at these qualities in more detail.

Detailed Appropriately

The product backlog items are detailed appropriately, as illustrated in Figure 3.1. Higher-priority items are described in more detail than lower-priority ones. "The lower the priority, the less detail, until you can barely make out the backlog item," write Schwaber and Beedle (2002, 33). Following this guideline keeps the backlog concise and ensures that the items likely to be implemented in the next sprint are workable. As a consequence, requirements are discovered, decomposed, and refined throughout the entire project.

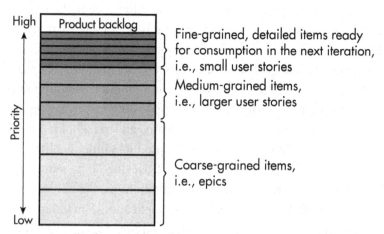

FIGURE 3.1 Product backlog prioritization determines the level of detail

---

1. I owe the acronym DEEP to Mike Cohn.

Estimated

The product backlog items are estimated. The estimates are coarse-grained and often expressed in story points or ideal days. Knowing the size of the items helps prioritize them and plan the release. (Detailed task-level estimations are created in the sprint planning meeting; tasks and their estimates are captured in the sprint backlog.)

Emergent

The product backlog has an organic quality. It evolves, and its contents change frequently. New items are discovered and added to the backlog based on customer and user feedback. Existing items are modified, reprioritized, refined, or removed on an ongoing basis.

Prioritized

All items in the product backlog are prioritized. The most important and highest-priority items are implemented first. They can be found at the top of the product backlog, as illustrated in Figure 3.1. Once an item is done, it is removed from the product backlog.

GROOMING THE PRODUCT BACKLOG

Like a garden growing wild when left unattended for too long, the product backlog becomes unwieldy when it's neglected. The backlog needs regular attention and care; it needs to be carefully managed, or groomed. Grooming the product backlog is an ongoing process that comprises the steps listed below. Note that these are not necessarily carried out in the order stated:

- New items are discovered and described, and existing ones are changed or removed as appropriate.
- The product backlog is prioritized. The most important items are now found at the top.

- The high-priority items are prepared for the upcoming sprint planning meeting; they are decomposed and refined.
- The team sizes product backlog items. Adding new items to the product backlog, changing existing ones, and correcting estimates make sizing necessary.

Although the product owner is responsible for making sure that the product backlog is in good shape, grooming is a collaborative process. Items are discovered and described, prioritized, decomposed, and refined by the entire Scrum team—Scrum allocates up to 10% of the team's availability for grooming activities (Schwaber 2007); stakeholders are involved as appropriate. Requirements are no longer handed off to the team; the team members coauthor them. The product owner, ScrumMaster, and team engage in face-to-face conversations rather than communicating via documents.

Grooming the product backlog collaboratively is fun and effective. It creates a dialogue within the Scrum team and between the team and the stakeholders. It removes the divide between "the business" and "the techies" and eliminates wasteful handoffs. It increases the clarity of the requirements, leverages the Scrum team's collective knowledge and creativity, and creates buy-in and joint ownership.

Some teams like to do a bit of grooming after their Daily Scrum. Others prefer weekly grooming sessions or a longer grooming workshop toward the end of the sprint. Grooming activities also take place in the sprint review meeting when the Scrum team and the stakeholders discuss the way forward; new backlog items are identified and old ones are removed. Make sure you establish a grooming process so that the activities are carried out reliably, for instance, by starting with weekly grooming workshops. A well-groomed backlog is a prerequisite for a successful sprint planning meeting.

There is a great tool to support product backlog grooming: paper cards. They are cheap and easy to use. They facilitate collaboration;

everyone can grab a card and write down an idea. They can also be grouped on the table or wall to check for consistency and completeness. Cards and electronic product backlog tools, such as spreadsheets, complement each other: Print out existing requirements on paper cards prior to a grooming workshop, and transfer the information on the cards back into the electronic tool afterward.

Let's now look closer at the four steps in the grooming process, beginning with discovering and describing product backlog items.

DISCOVERING AND DESCRIBING ITEMS

Discovering and describing product backlog items is an ongoing process. If you are used to creating comprehensive and detailed requirements specifications up front, recognize that Scrum encourages a fundamentally different approach. Requirements are no longer frozen early on but instead are discovered and detailed throughout the entire project. As our understanding of customer needs and how they can best be met improves, existing requirements are likely to change or become redundant, and new requirements will emerge. Product discovery is therefore not limited to the early development stages but covers the entire project in Scrum. Many product managers transitioning into the product owner role find it challenging not to write down all requirements and not to detail them straightaway—even if they could.

Discovering Items

Discovering product backlog items starts with stocking the product backlog. This is best done as a collaborative effort where the Scrum team and, as appropriate, stakeholders brainstorm the items necessary to bring the product to life, using the product idea, the product vision, or the product road map as a starting point. When stocking the product backlog, avoid the mistake of trying to think of every possible item. Whenever you work on the backlog, focus on the *minimum* functionality necessary to bring the product to life and strive for simplicity, as discussed in Chapter 2. As the project progresses, more ideas will emerge and the backlog will grow based on customer and user feedback. Starting with an overly long and complex product backlog makes it difficult to create focus and to prioritize items. Use the product idea or vision to guide your efforts. Focus only on what is critical and do not worry about the rest for now. Resist the temptation to add too much detail too quickly. Items are detailed progressively according to their priority. Low-priority items are large and coarse-grained. They stay like this until their priority changes (either because they are reprioritized or because higher-priority items have been consumed). Nonfunctional requirements that represent product-wide properties are the exception to this rule. These should be detailed early on, as I will explain later in this chapter.

Once the initial product backlog is in place, there are many opportunities to discover new items. These emerge in grooming workshops when the Scrum team prioritizes and decomposes product backlog items, they arise in the sprint review meetings when stakeholders give feedback, and they originate from customer and user comments on released product increments.

Whenever a requirement is entered into the backlog, ensure that the related customer need is properly understood. Ask why a requirement is necessary and how it benefits the customer. Do not make the mistake of blindly copying requirements into the product backlog, as this creates an inconsistent and unmanageable wish list. Treat existing requirements as suspicious and consider them as a liability, not an asset. A requirement simply describes product functionality that was thought to be necessary at some point in time. As markets and technologies change and as the Scrum team gains more knowledge about how customer needs can best be met, requirements also change or become obsolete.

Describing Items

Scrum does not mandate how product backlog items are described, but I prefer to work with user stories (Cohn 2004). As its name suggests, a user story tells a story about a customer or user employing the product. It contains a name, a brief narrative, and acceptance criteria, conditions that must hold true for the story to be complete. A story can be coarse-grained or detailed; coarse-grained stories are called *epics*. It's comparatively easy to write, decompose, and refine user stories. Of course, you are free to use any other technique to describe your requirements. And if you do use stories, you should not feel obligated to describe every single product backlog item as a user story. For instance, usability requirements are often best captured with prototypes or sketches.

Working with a product backlog does not mean that the Scrum team cannot create other helpful artifacts, including a summary of the various user roles, user story sequences to model workflows, diagrams to illustrate business rules, spreadsheets to capture complex calculations, user interface sketches, storyboards, user interface navigation diagrams, and user interface prototypes. These artifacts do not replace the product backlog but instead should elaborate and explain its content. And keep things simple. Only use artifacts that help the Scrum team move closer to a shippable product.

Structuring the Backlog

Product backlogs often benefit from grouping related items into themes. Themes act as placeholders for product functionality; they structure the backlog, aid prioritization, and make it easier to access information. Sample themes for a mobile phone are email, calendar, voice communication, and organizer, for instance. As a rule of thumb, each theme should contain between two and five coarse-grained requirements to start with. This tends to provide enough information to understand what it will take to bring the product to life without overspecifying the backlog contents. Themes create a hierarchy in the product backlog, which now contains groups in addition to individual items. Additionally, it can be useful to further distinguish between coarse-grained requirements, like epics, and detailed items, like stories, resulting in a product backlog as partially illustrated in Table 3.1.

TABLE 3.1 Sample Product Backlog

Theme	Coarse-Grained Item	Detailed Item	Effort
Email	Create email	As an enterprise user, I want to be able to state the email subject.	1

The themes in Table 3.1 contain coarse-grained items. Over time, these are decomposed into more detailed items. As the team estimates items, their size is recorded. Note that you can employ the structure in Table 3.1 independently of your product backlog tool, for instance, by appropriately arranging paper cards on a pin board, whiteboard, or the office wall.

PRIORITIZING THE PRODUCT BACKLOG

I'll never forget the day when I suggested to the product manager of a new health-care product to prioritize the use case pile in front of her. She looked at me, her eyes widening, and replied, "I can't. They are all high-priority."

Prioritization requires deciding how important an item is. If everything is high-priority, everything is equally important. This means in effect that nothing is a priority, so there is only a slim chance of delivering what the customer really needs. It's the product owner's responsibility to ensure that the product backlog is prioritized. Like the other grooming activities, prioritization is best carried out by the entire Scrum team. This leverages the team's collective knowledge and generates buy-in.

Prioritization directs the team's work by focusing the team on the most important items. It also freezes the backlog contents progressively. As mentioned before, items are detailed according to their priority. This builds flexibility into the process and allows delaying decisions about the lower-priority items, buying the Scrum team more time to evaluate options, gather feedback from customers, and acquire more knowledge. This ultimately results in better decisions and a better product.[2]

Since individual product backlog items can be very small and therefore difficult to prioritize, it's useful to prioritize themes first. We then prioritize the items within and, if necessary, across themes. The remainder of this section explores the following factors in prioritizing the product backlog: value; knowledge, uncertainty, and risk; releasability; and dependencies.

Value

Value is a common prioritization factor. We certainly want to deliver the most valuable items first. But what makes a product backlog item valuable? My answer is simple. An item is valuable if it is necessary for bringing the product to life. If that's not the case, the item is irrelevant; it is excluded from the current release or product version. The Scrum team either de-prioritizes the item and places it right at the bottom of the product backlog or better, discards it altogether. The latter keeps the product backlog concise and the Scrum team focused. If the item is important for a future version, it will reemerge.

Before including an item in the release, decide if the product could still achieve the desired benefits without that item. This helps

---

2. Delaying decisions until they have to be made is also referred to as the *last responsible moment* (Poppendieck 2003).

create a simple product, a product that implements the minimum functionality, as discussed in Chapter 2. Apple, for instance, shipped the first- and second-generation iPhone lacking a copy-and-paste functionality without damaging the product's success. If the item is indeed required, explore whether there is an alternative that achieves the same benefit but requires less effort or time or reduces unit cost. Even though this sounds like a no-brainer, teams can be constrained by hidden assumptions and do not always evaluate all relevant options.

Don't just scrutinize new requirements. Reexamine existing ones as well. Superior alternatives often arise after the Scrum team has learned more about customer needs and the solution being developed. Simplify, prune, and strive for order—like a gardener pulling out the weeds and trimming the shrubs.

When in doubt, exclude a requirement from the release and ship quickly without it—just as Google did when the company developed the first release of Google News, an application that aggregates news from around the world. The development team could not agree whether to filter the news by date or by location. So Google decided to release the new product without either feature. Shortly after the product's launch, requests for new features started to come in. Three hundred people requested filtering by date, while only three wanted to filter by location—a clear indication of which functionality should take priority. If Google had released the product with both features, the release would have consumed more time and money and it would have been harder to get feedback on which feature was more important. By putting out an intentionally insufficient product, Google quickly discovered what to do next.

Knowledge, Uncertainty, and Risk

"Risk is an essential characteristic of product innovation. Every decision regarding a project—whether made explicitly or implicitly—

has risk associated with it," write Smith and Merritt (2002, 4). Risk is therefore an intrinsic part of software development; no product can come to life risk-free. Correlated with risk is uncertainty. The more uncertainty there is, the riskier the project is. Uncertainty, in turn, is caused by a lack of knowledge. The less we know about what to develop and how to do it, the more uncertainty is present. Knowledge, uncertainty, and risk are therefore interlinked.

Because risk and uncertainty influence product success, uncertain and risky items should be high-priority. This accelerates the generation of new knowledge, drives out uncertainty, and reduces risk. If the Scrum team, for instance, is unsure about some aspects of the user interface design, the relevant design options should be explored and tested by gathering feedback from customers and users. If the team does not know whether a third-party database access layer should be used, requirements triggering database transactions should be implemented early so that the different options can be evaluated. Note that risk can also hide in the infrastructure and environment, including a build process not yet set up or the Scrum team not being colocated.

Tackling uncertain, risky items early creates a risk-driven approach that may enforce early failure. Failing early allows the Scrum team to change course while there is still the opportunity, for instance, to modify the architecture and technology selection, or to adjust the team composition. A risk-driven, fail-early approach can be difficult to accept for individuals and organizations used to traditional processes, where problems and impediments surface late in the game and are often perceived as bad news rather than an opportunity to learn and improve.

Releasability

Releasing early and frequently is a great way to let the software evolve into a product that customers love, as discussed in Chapter 4.

It's also an effective way to mitigate risks. If the Scrum team is uncertain about if and how a feature should be implemented, early releases can answer this question, as in the case of Google News discussed earlier.

Being able to release product increments early and frequently should therefore influence the product backlog prioritization. Each release should provide functionality that is useful to customers and users and that generates the desired feedback. Note that it's usually not necessary to fully implement a theme; a partial implementation is often sufficient for early releases.

Dependencies

Whether we like it or not, dependencies in the product backlog are a fact. Functional requirements, for instance, often depend on other functional and even nonfunctional requirements. And if several teams work together, dependencies between them can influence the prioritization, as further discussed in Chapter 4. Dependencies restrict the freedom to prioritize the product backlog and influence the effort estimates; the item on which others depend has to be implemented first. You should therefore try to resolve dependencies whenever possible.

Combining several dependent items into one larger one and splitting the items differently are two common techniques for dealing with dependent user stories (Cohn 2004, 17). Let's look at two sample stories: "As a user I want to write a text message" and "As a user I want to write an email message." They are dependent because both stories require a text-processing capability. If we implement the text message story first, the effort of the email message story is reduced, and vice versa. The first option is to combine them into a larger story. This is not appealing because it would result in a big compound story. The second option is to slice the requirements differently. If the common functionality is extracted into a separate story—"As a user, I want to enter text"—the two original stories are no longer dependent on each other. As such, their estimates are no longer influenced by the order in which they are worked on.

GETTING READY FOR SPRINT PLANNING

Prior to each sprint planning meeting, the product backlog items that are likely to be worked on in the next sprint have to be prepared. We begin the preparation work by choosing a sprint goal.

Choosing a Sprint Goal

The sprint goal summarizes the desired outcome of the sprint. It should move the Scrum team a step closer toward the launch of a successful product. The product owner on a project I worked with selected the following goal for the first sprint: "Tall trees have deep roots." The goal nicely described the purpose of the sprint: laying the foundation for the remainder of the project. A good sprint goal is broad but realistic. It should leave some room for the team to maneuver and still be valid if the team does not commit to all the top product backlog items. As with all grooming activities, the team should participate in formulating the goal. This ensures clarity and buy-in.

Sprint goals are beneficial for several reasons:

- They create alignment among the product owner, ScrumMaster, and team: Everyone is working toward a common goal.
- They minimize variation by limiting the type of requirements worked on in a given sprint, for instance, by choosing items from the same theme. This facilitates close teamwork and can help increase velocity.
- They make it easier to communicate to stakeholders what the team is working on.

Note that choosing a sprint goal can lead to adjustments of the product backlog's prioritization, including promoting and demoting items to and from the top. You might have to make a trade-off between choosing a cohesive sprint goal and getting items worked on quickly. Once the goal has been set, all relevant items should be found at the top of the product backlog.

Preparing Just Enough Items Just in Time

Once a sprint goal is chosen, we prepare just enough items for the upcoming sprint, just in time.[3] (I discuss large projects that require looking ahead farther later in this chapter.) The grooming activities in the first sprint focus on the items for the second sprint, and those in the second sprint on the items for the third, and so on. This approach has a number of benefits: It minimizes the amount of time and money spent on describing product backlog items, and it keeps the inventory of detailed items low—providing more information than required is wasteful. By detailing only the items that are likely to be chosen for the upcoming sprint, we allow the product backlog to evolve.

Getting the items ready for the sprint planning meeting requires decomposing larger product backlog items until they are small enough to fit into a sprint and refining the items so that they are clear, feasible, and testable. Figure 3.2 illustrates this process. Note that decomposing items can take several sprints, as I will discuss shortly.

How many items should be prepared depends on the team's velocity and the desired granularity of the items. The higher the team's velocity, the more items have to be prepared. It is helpful to groom a few extra items to give the team some flexibility. They also come in handy when the team's sprint progress is faster than anticipated. I find it beneficial to work with small requirements that can be "done" within a few days, independent of the sprint length. This

---

3. The terms *just enough* and *just in time* were first used in Cohn (2008) to discuss grooming activities.

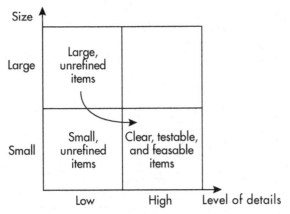

FIGURE 3.2 Decomposing and refining product backlog items

improves the team's progress tracking within the sprint and therefore its self-organization: A team's progress is based not only on its remaining tasks but also on how much newly implemented functionality has been tested and documented. Small requirements also minimize the amount of work in progress and the risk of partially done and defective work at the end of the sprint. In addition, small items facilitate realistic commitments. Large ones can contain so many tasks that the team might fail to identify them all.

Decomposing Items

Decomposing product backlog items means making them smaller and smaller until they fit into a sprint. This process, also known as *progressive requirements decomposition* (Reinertsen 1997), might last more than one sprint. You might have to start decomposing a product backlog item a few sprints in advance before it can be implemented, particularly if the item is large and complex. This allows gathering the necessary feedback from customers, users, and other stakeholders before detailing the item. Let's look at how user stories can be decomposed progressively.

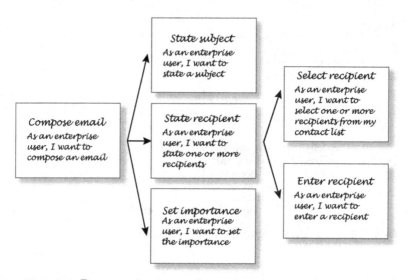

FIGURE 3.3 Decomposing user stories

As illustrated in Figure 3.3, the Scrum team originally placed the epic "Compose email" in the product backlog. As it is too big and vague to be delivered in a sprint, the epic is broken down into several coarse-grained user stories. The story "State recipient" is then further decomposed into two fine-grained user stories. These are now small enough to fit in a sprint. The epic is an example of a compound story, a user story that has more than one goal (Cohn 2004, 24–25). To decompose such a story, we introduce a separate story for each goal. "Compose email" is therefore broken into "State subject," "State recipient," and "Set importance."

There are other user stories that need to be decomposed, including complex stories and stories with monster criteria. A complex user story is a story that is too big to be delivered in one sprint because of its inherent uncertainty or because it covers too much functionality (Cohn 2004, 25–26). If it is too uncertain, we introduce one or more items into the product backlog that explore that uncertainty and generate the relevant knowledge: for instance, "Investigate JavaServer Faces as the user interface technology." If the story describes too much functionality, we split it into several stories to allow incremental delivery of the functionality. This technique is also called *slicing the cake* (Cohn 2004, 76). A story that says, for instance, "Validate the user" could be decomposed into "Validate the user name" and "Validate the password."

Stories sometimes look fine until we consider the acceptance criteria. If there are too many—more than about ten—or if requirements hide in the criteria, we need to rework and decompose the story. Here is an example: "As a user, I want to delete a text message." The acceptance criteria state, "I can select any text message. I can remove the message text. I can save the modified message." Not only is the second condition redundant, but the other two introduce new requirements rather than specifying acceptance criteria. This story should be split into three: a story about deleting text messages, a story about editing text messages, and another story about saving the modified messages.

Ensuring Clarity, Testability, and Feasibility

Once an item is small enough, we must ensure that it is clear, testable, and feasible.[4] A requirement is *clear* if all Scrum team members have a common understanding of its semantics. Collaboratively describing requirements and expressing backlog items in a simple and concise form facilitate clarity. An item is *testable* if there is an effective way to determine whether the requirement is satisfied within the sprint in which it is implemented. Stories must have acceptance criteria now to ensure that each story is testable. An item is *feasible* if it can be completed in one sprint, according to the team's definition of done. (The definition of done is discussed in Chapter 5.) To ensure feasibility we

---

4. Bill Wake has suggested that stories should be independent, negotiable, valuable, estimatable, small, and testable, also referred to as the INVEST criteria (Wake 2003). Dependencies and value are discussed in the prioritization section; estimation is also covered in this chapter. Negotiability refers to the ability to adjust a user story. A story is a promise for a conversation, as Ron Jeffries has said, and not a hard-and-fast requirement.

consider dependencies on other items, including functional and nonfunctional requirements. If a story is constrained by a user interface requirement, for instance, it must be clear what the resulting product increment should look like. If that is not the case, the team should explore the user interface requirement before the story is implemented. If exploring the item requires a large effort, the exploration should be tackled in a separate sprint, for instance, by implementing a throwaway prototype to investigate the user interface design.

SIZING ITEMS

Estimating product backlog items allows us to understand their rough size and the likely effort necessary to provide them. That's helpful for two reasons: It facilitates prioritization, and it allows us to track and forecast the project's progress. Note that there are two distinct estimates in Scrum: coarse-grained estimates in the product backlog indicating the rough size of an item, and fine-grained estimates in the sprint backlog communicating the size of a task, usually stated in hours. This section discusses sizing the items in the product backlog. Product backlog items are estimated when new items are discovered or existing ones are modified, and when the team's understanding of an item's size changes. We consequently need a measure that is quick and easy to use. My favorite one is story points.[5]

Story Points

Story points are coarse-grained, relative measures of raw effort and size.[6] An item worth one story point is half the size of an item worth two points. An item sized as three points requires as much effort as

---

5. See Cohn (2005) for a more detailed and comprehensive discussion of estimation techniques.

6. Time is captured separately from effort by velocity as discussed in Chapter 4.

an item with one point and an item with two points added together. Relative measures take advantage of the fact that size itself is relative; the semantics of big and small depend on our reference point. My computer mouse is small compared to my laptop but big compared to the memory stick next to it. A commonly used range of story points is listed in Table 3.2.

TABLE 3.2 A Popular Story Point Range

Story Point	T-shirt Size	
0	Freebie, item has already been implemented	
1	XS	Extra small
2	S	Small
3	M	Medium
5	L	Large
8	XL	Extra-large
13	XXL	Double extra-large
20	XXXL	Huge

The nonlinear sequence in Table 3.2 speeds up the team's decision-making process. It prevents lengthy discussions about the "right value" that can arise when linear sequences are used. The team can extend the range shown in Table 3.2, adding 40 and 100 as larger values, as long as the relative estimates are correct. Whatever the range it chooses, the team should feel comfortable with the sequence and stick to it. Because story points are relative and arbitrary, they cannot be compared across teams unless the teams have agreed on a common range with common semantics.

Planning Poker

Story points alone are great but are not enough. We need a technique to enable effective team-based estimation. Planning Poker is such a technique (Cohn 2005, 56–59). In Planning Poker, every team member is given a deck of cards that contains all of the agreed-upon story point values. If we were using the range in Table 3.2, for instance, the deck would include eight cards, each displaying one of the story points in the range. Once all cards have been dealt to the participants, the estimation starts.

If this is the first time the team has sized backlog items, the team will need to determine what the values in the range mean to them. To do this, many teams choose a product backlog item that they can all agree is small and use it as the first one they estimate. Alternatively, the team can select the smallest, the largest, and a medium-sized item and estimate them in turn. If, on the other hand, the team is familiar with the range, they typically start with the highest-priority item and work their way down.

Before the team estimates, the product owner explains the item to the team members, who then briefly discuss the steps to deliver the item according to the definition of done. After the discussion, each team member sizes the item privately, without making any assumptions about who might implement the item, as that's not decided until the relevant Daily Scrum. Each team member chooses the card with the right estimate and puts it facedown on the table. After everyone has played a card, the cards are all turned over at the same time. If the estimates differ, the two team members whose estimates are farthest apart briefly explain their reasoning. The team then plays another round. All cards are returned to the decks, and team members again choose the card that best matches their estimate, which may or may not have changed after the first round. This cycle continues until the estimates converge. The decision-making rule is consensus; all team members should be comfortable with the estimate. As soon as the team has estimated more than two items, the new estimates should be compared against existing ones to ensure that the relative size is correct, for instance, by grouping items with the same size.

Estimating Nonfunctional Requirements

Nonfunctional requirements that apply to all functional require-ments, such as performance or user experience requirements, are usually not estimated separately. Instead, they are included in the team's definition of done. If, however, dedicated work is required to implement a nonfunctional requirement, such as exploring differ-ent user interface design options or carrying out architecture refac-toring, the relevant items should be placed in the product backlog and sized by the team. Including nonfunctional requirements in the definition of done does not mean they come for free. The opposite is true; the definition of done influences the team's estimates.

To achieve reasonably accurate estimates, three things are required: The team must roughly know what it takes to deliver an item, its members must be able to determine dependencies on other items, and a definition of done must be available. If the team is not in a position to estimate the item, it should add a new item to the back-log that will generate the relevant knowledge, for instance, "Create a prototype or mock-up to explore user interface design options."

Only team members who create product increments should be allowed to estimate the product backlog items. The product owner and ScrumMaster should not estimate, nor should they influ-ence the estimates (unless they are performers on the team or the team asks for advice). The product owner must, however, be present at the meeting. Many product backlog items will be sketchy, and the product owner will need to explain and clarify them.

Fast-Track Estimation

If the team is too pressed for time to use Planning Poker, consider using the following estimation technique. Divide one wall of the meeting room into several sections, each labeled with a different number in the story point range. Print the product backlog items on paper cards and place them on a table. Have each team member take one card, decide on an estimate, and then place the card on the section of the wall that corresponds to its story size, making sure that the item corresponds to the size of the other items in the same group. If anyone spots a card that does not fit, he or she should immediately move it to the right group. This process generates estimates for many backlog items very quickly, with minimal effort. Its main drawback is that the team does not have a conversation about the size of the items. The quality of the estimates, therefore, tends to be lower compared to the Planning Poker results.

DEALING WITH NONFUNCTIONAL REQUIREMENTS

Nonfunctional requirements—also called operational requirements, qualities of the system, and constraints—are software development's ugly ducklings. They are often neglected even though they describe important properties, such as performance, robustness, scalability, usability, as well as technical and compliance requirements (for instance, supporting a protocol or the ability to gain certification). They influence user interface design, architecture, and technology choices, impacting the total cost of ownership and the product's life expectancy. This section explores describing and managing nonfunctional requirements in Scrum.

Describing Nonfunctional Requirements

Nonfunctional requirements can be expressed as *constraints* (Newkirk and Martin 2001, 16–18). We could, for instance, describe a performance requirement as shown in Figure 3.4.

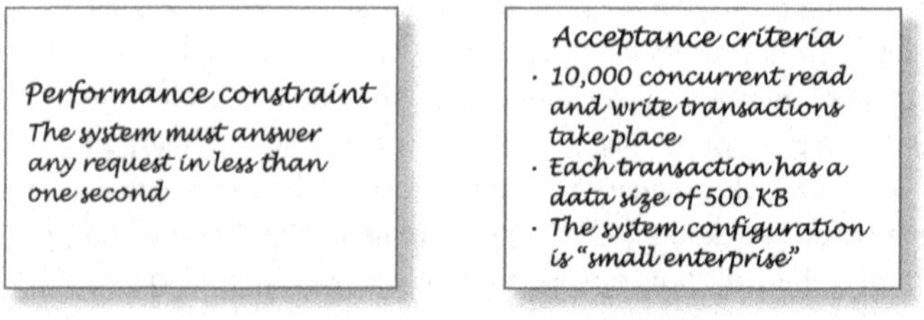

Performance constraint
The system must answer any request in less than one second

Acceptance criteria
· 10,000 concurrent read and write transactions take place
· Each transaction has a data size of 500 KB
· The system configuration is "small enterprise"

FIGURE 3.4 Nonfunctional requirement formulated as a constraint

User experience requirements are often best captured as sketches, storyboards, user interface navigation diagrams, and prototypes. My experience suggests that teams prefer these artifacts to user interface guidelines in textual form.

Managing Nonfunctional Requirements

When managing nonfunctional requirements, it's helpful to distinguish between global and local requirements. The former relate to all functional requirements and usually form a small group. An example is the performance constraint shown in Figure 3.4. Global nonfunctional requirements should be detailed early on—when creating the vision or when stocking the product backlog. Discovering and refining them too late can cause wrong choices and negatively impact product success. Global nonfunctional requirements can be captured in a separate area of the product backlog, as illustrated in Table 3.3.

TABLE 3.3 Sample Product Backlog with Nonfunctional Requirements

Functional Requirements				Nonfunctional Requirements
Theme	Coarse-Grained Requirement	Detailed Requirement	Effort	
Email	Create email	As an enterprise user, I want to be able to state the email subject.	1	The product must answer any request in less than one second.

It is often useful to incorporate global nonfunctional requirements in the definition of done. As a consequence, every product increment has to fulfill these requirements.

In contrast to their global siblings, local nonfunctional requirements apply only to a specific functional requirement, for instance, a specific performance requirement for retrieving information. If the nonfunctional requirement is expressed as a constraint, we can simply attach the constraint to the story, as suggested by Newkirk and Martin (2001) and Cohn (2004). This can be done by annotating the story with the constraint.

SCALING THE PRODUCT BACKLOG

Large projects bring new challenges. One of them is how to scale the product backlog. To succeed, employ one product backlog, extend the grooming horizon, and consider providing team-specific views into the backlog.

Use One Product Backlog

Whenever you work on a large Scrum project, ensure that there is one product backlog that contains the work necessary to bring the product to life. Avoid team- or component-specific backlogs that translate product requirements into subsystem or component requirements. They create significant overhead, as their contents have to be derived from the product backlog; they also have to be groomed and kept in sync. Try to feed all teams directly from the product backlog and prefer feature teams to component teams, as discussed in Chapter 1. Darin Fisher, one of the engineers on the Chrome browser project, describes what Google did to keep its large project working from one product backlog: "When it came to requirements, a lot of the process involved brainstorming meetings with the team and we talked about features. We also had an open mail list internally at Google where people said what would be cool.... We tried to keep the features very focused and minimal. Then we shared the list with the whole team, and people would self-select for what they wanted to work on."[7]

---

7. Interview with Darin Fisher by Colleen Frye on SearchSoftwareQuality.com on October 1, 2008.

Extend the Grooming Horizon

Product backlog items are still decomposed and refined just in time on large Scrum projects. But the grooming horizon changes. Rather than focusing on the subsequent sprint, large projects look ahead to the next two to three sprints when preparing the product backlog, as discussed in Chapter 4. Consequently, there is a bigger inventory of detailed product backlog items on a large Scrum project than on a small one.

Provide Separate Backlog Views

Large agile projects with many feature teams can benefit from using separate views into the product backlog (Cohn 2009, 330–31). Each view shows a subset of the product backlog. If a feature team works on the theme "organizer" in the next few sprints, for instance, the team's view into the backlog consists of the corresponding backlog subset. Views can prevent conflicts between several product owners and teams all working on the same product backlog.

COMMON MISTAKES

Although the product backlog is a beautifully simple tool, it can be difficult to use it well. Watch out for the following common mistakes: a requirements spec dressed up as a backlog, a wish list for Santa, pushing requirements onto the team, neglecting product backlog grooming, and feeding a team with several backlogs.

Disguised Requirements Specification

A requirements specification dressed up as a product backlog is like the devil in disguise: It looks neat, pretty, and perfect. It is tempting because it appeals to our old desire to know all the requirements up front. But it has a hidden dark side. A product backlog that is too detailed and too comprehensive does not support the emergence of requirements. It does not view requirements as fluid and transient but rather as fixed and definite; it freezes all decisions about how customer needs can be satisfied at an early point in time.

A requirements specification disguised as a product backlog is likely to be a symptom of an unhealthy relationship between the product owner and the team. If you encounter such a backlog, see if a product vision is available. If it is, derive a new product backlog from the vision and discard the disguised requirements spec. If no product vision exists, stop and carry out the necessary visioning work. You can, of course, choose to plod along, wrestle with the backlog, extract themes, rewrite items as user stories, and struggle to prioritize the backlog. But this is unlikely to maximize your chances of launching a winning product.

Wish List for Santa

A product backlog that resembles a child's wish list for Santa contains anything and everything we have thought of that we might ever need. This backlog is no longer a queue of outstanding work; it is instead a requirements database. A wish list for a backlog is not only notoriously difficult to prioritize; it also limits the product's ability to evolve based on customer and user feedback, as too much functionality has already been identified. Use the product idea or vision to determine which items are critical for developing and launching a successful product. Discard the rest.

Requirements Push

Sometimes, the product owner writes the backlog items alone and then hands them off to the team in the sprint planning meeting. This approach reinforces the old them-and-us divide: the product owner here, the team over there. It wastes the team's knowledge, experience, and creativity and makes sprint planning more difficult. Make sure the product owner always involves fellow Scrum team members in the grooming work. Set up one or more grooming workshops per sprint, invite the rest of the Scrum team, and remind the team to allocate time for the grooming work in every sprint. Always remember the Agile Manifesto's collaboration mantra: "Business people and developers must work together daily throughout the project" (Beck et. al. 2001).

Grooming Neglect

Most sprint planning meetings I have attended were fun. The ones that weren't involved a poorly groomed product backlog. When the backlog isn't groomed prior to the meeting, the product owner and team often try to carry out impromptu grooming activities, which consume valuable planning time and result in poor requirements and weak commitments. Plus, everyone is exhausted by the end of the meeting. Recognize that if the product backlog is not properly groomed, the next sprint should not start. It should be postponed until the backlog has been prepared.

Competing Backlogs

A client of mine once had five product owners working with one team. Because each product owner wanted to get as much work done as quickly as possible, the team was asked to work on all five backlogs in every sprint. This gave the product owners a certain comfort level; they knew their requirements were being worked on. It also left them very dissatisfied; it took ages to get anything done. Working on multiple products concurrently may look good. Everyone is busy. Everything is being worked on. But nothing progresses quickly. Instead, this team never has a cohesive sprint goal and wastes valuable time with task switching.

If your team has to work on several product backlogs, make sure every sprint focuses on only one product. Even better, ask the team to work on just one product for a few sprints so they can release a new product version quickly. Then move on to the next product. This approach requires prioritizing the products and establishing a portfolio management process. My client's issue ultimately resided with the company's CEO, who wanted everything done by yesterday and found it difficult to set priorities to guide the product owners.

REFLECTION

Believe in your creativity and allow the product backlog content to emerge. Keep your backlog simple and concise. Focus on the items that are essential for bringing the product to life. Be courageous and weed out items. The following questions will help you apply the concepts described in this chapter:

How are requirements discovered and described in your workplace?

Does your product backlog exhibit the DEEP characteristics?

How is your product backlog groomed?

What would it take to discover and describe requirements collaboratively in every sprint?

How do you deal with nonfunctional requirements? When and how are they captured?

4
· · ·

PLANNING THE RELEASE

"Planning ... is a quest for value," writes Mike Cohn (Cohn 2005, 5), and release planning supports the development and launch of a successful product. It facilitates a dialogue between the Scrum team and the stakeholders, and it answers the question of which functionality the project is likely to deliver by when. Release planning takes place throughout the project, as the team listens and responds to customer and user feedback. Shifting from document-driven planning and reporting to conversation and dialogue allows the Scrum team to use simple planning techniques, which makes planning itself simpler and more transparent. Even though release planning is a collaborative effort, the product owner is responsible for ensuring that the necessary decisions are made.

This chapter discusses essential release planning concepts and techniques. For a more comprehensive and detailed discussion, refer to *Agile Estimating and Planning* (Cohn 2005).

TIME, COST, AND FUNCTIONALITY

Release planning starts with making a decision about which project lever—time, cost, or functionality—cannot be compromised to launch a successful product. Is adherence to the launch date mandatory? Is the development budget fixed? Or do all product requirements in the product backlog have to be delivered? Fixing time, budget, *and* functionality is not possible; at least one of the three levers has to act as a release valve. Here is my recommendation: Fix time and flex functionality.

Fixing functionality is a bad idea. Even with a product vision in place, the product's exact properties, its functionality and features, are not all known up front but are instead discovered based on customer and user feedback. Requirements emerge and the product backlog evolves as the Scrum team learns more about customer needs and how to meet them. Trying to fix functionality severely damages the team's ability to adapt the product to the customer's response. It is likely to result in a poor product—and not a product that customers love.

Identifying the launch date is facilitated by the product vision. The vision allows us to determine the window of opportunity, the time frame in which the product must be launched to achieve the desired benefits. Fixing the window of opportunity protects time as the scarcest resource. If the date is missed, the opportunity is gone, and launching the product no longer makes sense. Note that choosing a launch date based on the work in the product backlog is difficult, as it forces the team to freeze requirements and often results in a poor estimate. In fact, an estimated launch date based on requirements may be off by as much as 60 to 160%; a project expected to take 20 weeks could take anywhere from 12 to 32 weeks (Cohn 2005, 4). This well-known correlation is called the Cone of Uncertainty.[1] Identifying the window of

---

1. The Cone of Uncertainty was first recognized by Barry Boehm.

opportunity rather than trying to estimate a probable launch date avoids these issues.

Fixing the date provides the opportunity to create a steady innovation cadence. This is achieved by choosing the same timebox for all releases. Sound crazy? Well, that's what Salesforce.com, a leading provider of on-demand customer relationship management services, did—with quite some success. After years of rapid growth, Salesforce.com found itself in a difficult situation in 2006. Its ability to release new products had decreased to only one per year, and productivity had sharply declined. In an effort to turn around its fortunes, the company introduced Scrum. Chris Fry, vice president of platform development at Salesforce.com, explains:[2]

> The decision to go agile at Salesforce.com grew out of a desire to create shorter more predictable releases. We had gone a year without a major release and wanted to get onto a more predictable release schedule that would deliver value at a consistent rate to our customers.

Since introducing Scrum, Salesforce.com has followed a strict innovation cadence. "The entire organization has moved from a 12-month cycle to a four-month rhythm, delivering three major releases per year all on schedule. This includes all product software development, technical operations, and internal IT systems," states Steve Greene, vice president of program management and agile development at Salesforce.com[3] The results are stunning. Salesforce.com experienced an amazing 97% increase in the number of features delivered by establishing short, steady release cycles. At the same time, the company managed to reduce its lead time for new functionality by 61%. Estimating and planning have also become more effective and accurate. It's now easier for Salesforce.com's customers to plan for the next release. At

---

2. Interview with Chris Fry, www.agilethinkers.com/chris_fry_salesforcecom_qa/.

3. Personal communication with Steve Greene on April 16, 2009.

the same time, the development teams are happier, too (Greene and Fry 2008).

Fixing the date and using stable Scrum teams make determining a budget straightforward—assuming that labor is the decisive cost factor. If you have to scale your project, accurately forecasting the budget is more difficult, particularly for new-product development projects. If the budget is in danger of getting overrun, the product owner has to make a choice: Either ship with less functionality, or increase cost by asking more people to join the project—as long as there is enough time for the new project members to increase productivity. Apple, for instance, decided to increase cost and added more people to its first iPhone project in order to stick to the release date. But beware of Brooks's Law: "Adding manpower to a late software project makes it later" (Brooks 1995, 25).

What about Fixed-Price Contracts?

If you have a choice, avoid projects with fixed price and fixed scope. If that's not possible, try the following: Split a fixed-price contract into two parts and carry out two consecutive projects. The first project creates the product vision and partly implements the vision using two to three sprints. At the end of the project, the product backlog has evolved based on customer feedback. This enables you to create a realistic release plan and to come up with a realistic budget estimate for the second project, which continues to bring the product to life. Recognize that Scrum is a disruptive process innovation. As with any disruptive innovation, your existing clients and customers may not be willing to embrace the innovation; in their minds, they already have a solution that seems to work.

QUALITY IS FROZEN

As we've seen, the product's functionality evolves. Its fidelity can also increase during the project: The look and feel and the overall user experience might improve. But the software quality is frozen in

Scrum. The quality criteria are captured in the definition of done. This definition usually requires that a (potentially) shippable product increment be available at the end of each sprint: executable software that has been tested and documented and that could be released. Quality assurance and control measures form an integral part of the sprints—instead of being carried out at the end of the project as an afterthought.

It is crucial to ensure that sprints do deliver increments with the right quality. The product owner should not encourage the team to make compromises to the software quality and should never accept work results that do not fulfill the done criteria. Quality compromises result in defective product increments, making it impossible to clearly see the progress and to release early and frequently. To make things worse, compromising quality has negative long-term effects. It creates technical debt, software that is difficult to extend and maintain (Cunningham 1992). It can damage the brand and leave customers dissatisfied. Compromising software quality means trading in short-term gains for longer-term growth. You would cheat yourself of a better, brighter future.

EARLY AND FREQUENT RELEASES

"Our highest priority is to satisfy the customer through early and continuous delivery of valuable software," states the Manifesto for Agile Software Development, and recommends, "Deliver working software frequently, from a couple of weeks to a couple of months, with a preference to the shorter timescale" (Beck et al. 2001). Releasing product increments to target customers early and frequently—instead of delivering the finished product in one go—provides invaluable feedback.[4]

---

4. Early and frequent releases are an old idea; they date back at least to Tom Gilb's evolutionary delivery method (Gilb 1988). Extreme programming also promotes frequent releases called *short releases* in Beck (2000) and *incremental deployment* in Beck and Andres (2005).

It lets the product evolve based on the customer response. It saves the Scrum team from implementing the wrong features and from creating a product with too much or too little functionality. This helps develop a product that is *just right*.

Frequent releases are so powerful because customers and users can employ the product in its target environment rather than just viewing a demo in the sprint review meeting. What's more, releasing early and often allows the Scrum team to reach out to a larger group of people, reducing the risk of selecting the wrong target customers. Releasing software early provides another advantage: It quickly reveals an ill-conceived vision, providing the opportunity to revise the vision or to cancel the project at an early stage.

The team developing the Google Chrome browser, for instance, first thought it could leave out the bookmark bar altogether. But user feedback showed that some people love to navigate by clicking on the bookmark bar. So the team came up with a new solution: If the user has previously configured the bar in Internet Explorer or Firefox, Chrome will import the setup. Otherwise, users won't have a bookmark bar unless they choose to. Without releasing early versions of the browser, the team might not have discovered the bookmark bar's importance and would have ended up shipping a suboptimal product. In fact, frequent releases form a building block of Google's innovation capability, as Bernard Girard, author of *The Google Way*, observes: "By bringing products to market rapidly, whether they're ready or not, Google derives maximum benefit from its efforts and short-circuits potential competition ... Google's strategy of releasing early and often is also a brilliant and inventive marketing strategy: It dissuades potential competitors, raises the cost of entry to the market, and keeps users in Google's sphere of influence" (Girard 2009, 86).

As with all things, there is no free lunch. Frequent releases do have a price: The software must be of high quality, and the product must be easy to obtain and install. It's perfectly OK to have some features that are implemented only partially in early product increments. It is also acceptable to release functionality that provides only limited benefits to a customer or user. But the software quality, as defined in the definition of done, must be right with all product increments. This allows the team to quickly adapt the product in future sprints, and it prevents bugs that damage the product's reputation. Agile development practices such as test-driven development and test automation, refactoring, and continuous integration facilitate the creation of shippable product increments. Teams will need time to learn these useful practices, and applying them might require infrastructure and environment changes.

If it's not easy to obtain and install new product versions, customers will reject or ignore updates. Although this can be challenging to achieve, "any large project can be broken down into a series of smaller and earlier deliverables. Don't give up, even if you have to change the technical solution to make it happen. Keep your eyes on the results, not the technologies" (Gilb 1988, 336).

QUARTERLY CYCLES

There is no rule in Scrum that mandates how long a project can last. But it is common for agile projects to take no longer than three to six months. If you need more than three or four months to bring the product to life, you should use quarterly cycles, releasing at least one version of working, tested, and documented software each quarter (see Beck and Andres 2005, 47–48). Google took advantage of quarterly cycles during the two years it needed to develop the first version of its Chrome browser. Darin Fisher describes the process: "We oriented things around quarters, so the living document [the product backlog] was revised each quarter; say this quarter we're focusing on this subset, etc. It was helpful to drive the product forward, and to make sure the product very early on was usable by anybody at Google so we'd have continuous feedback."[5] Another company that systematically employs quarterly releases is PatientKeeper, Inc., a provider of health-care products. The company launches a new product version every three months (Sutherland 2005). Bearing in mind that PatientKeeper's products are safety-critical, need FDA approval, and are deployed into heterogeneous hospital environments, this is a major achievement that equips the company with a significant competitive advantage. It is no coincidence that PatientKeeper has established itself as a leader in health-care mobile applications, keeping even much larger competitors at bay.

VELOCITY

Velocity is an indicator of how much work the team can do in a sprint; it allows us to track and forecast the project's progress. More precisely, velocity is the sum of the effort for the work results accepted by the product owner in a sprint. Let's look at an example. In the sprint planning meeting, a team commits to deliver six stories with a total effort of 12 story points. Now at the end of the sprint, the product owner carefully inspects the increment and discovers that all requirements have been delivered according to the definition of done but one: A minor part of the documentation of story D has not been completed. Because D is not complete, its story points do not count toward the team velocity, as depicted in Table 4.1. The sum of the story points for the accepted backlog items is 10. The team's velocity for this sprint is, therefore, 10 points.

---

5. Interview with Darin Fisher by Colleen Frye on SearchSoftwareQuality.com on October 1, 2008.

TABLE 4.1 Determining Velocity

Product Backlog Item	Story Points	Review Result
A	1	Accepted
B	3	Accepted
C	1	Accepted
D	2	Rejected
E	2	Accepted
F	3	Accepted

As illustrated in the example, velocity is best determined by observing the team's ability to turn product backlog items into product increments. "Working software is the primary measure of progress," as the Manifesto for Agile Software Development puts it (Beck et al. 2001). Note that velocity can vary, as a number of factors, including team-building dynamics, impediments, and availability, influence it. If several team members take time off, for instance, the velocity is likely to drop. And on new teams or on new-product development projects the velocity can take two to three sprints to stabilize (Cohn 2005, 179).

Velocity is specific to a team and, generally speaking, cannot be compared across teams—unless the teams use story points with the same meaning. Knowing that team one developing product A has a velocity of 40 and team two developing product B has a velocity of 20 does *not* mean that team one is more productive. Team one might have lower estimates than team two.

THE RELEASE BURNDOWN

The release burndown is the bread-and-butter artifact for tracking and forecasting the project progress in Scrum. It comes in two flavors: as a burndown chart and a burndown bar. Let's look at the release burndown chart first.

The Release Burndown Chart

The release burndown chart allows us to track and forecast project progress (Schwaber and Beedle 2002, 83–88). Based on the velocity of the past sprints, the release burndown anticipates the future so that the Scrum team can adapt the product and project as needed.[6] It is based on the following two factors: the remaining effort in the product backlog, and time. The chart is best created and updated in the sprint review meeting, when the sprint outcome is known.

Creating the release burndown is simple. First, we draw a coordinate system and choose the number of sprints as the unit on the x-axis. On the y-axis, we write the story points (or any other effort measure you use). The first data point is the estimated effort of the entire product backlog before any development has taken place. To arrive at our next data point, we determine the remaining effort in the product backlog at the end of the first sprint. Then we draw a line through the two points. This line is called the *burndown*. It shows the rate at which the effort in the product backlog is consumed. If we extend the burndown line to the x-axis, we can forecast when the project is likely to finish—assuming effort and velocity stay stable. Let's have a look at a sample burndown chart, shown in Figure 4.1.

The release burndown chart in Figure 4.1 shows two lines. The solid line is the actual burndown. It documents the progress to date and the effort remaining. We can see at a glance that the project has experienced a rather slow start. This might be caused by impediments and risks materializing, team-building dynamics, or technology issues. In the third sprint, the remaining effort even increased. This may have been caused by the team reestimating backlog items or discovering new requirements necessary to fulfill

---

6. Beck and Fowler (2000) refer to this property as *yesterday's weather*. Note that a rough forecast is acceptable since the progress is inspected every few weeks in the sprint review meeting, providing a new opportunity to update the release burndown and adapt the forecast.

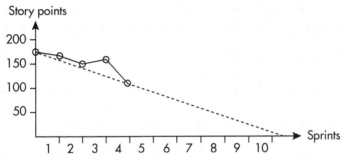

FIGURE 4.1 Release burndown chart

the vision. The fourth sprint saw a steep burndown; the project progressed fast. If we now reflect on the past sprints, we can create a burndown trend, depicted as a dashed line in Figure 4.1. The burndown trend forecasts the progress in the next sprints. It shows that, if the work in the product backlog and the rate of progress stay constant, the project will not be complete within ten sprints—the project is off track. Equipped with this knowledge, the Scrum team can investigate the causes. Is the progress too slow, or is there too much work? Once the team is clear on the cause, it can take the right action. Assuming the date is fixed, the team might reduce functionality or request that a specialist be added to the team, for instance.

The burndown chart must be used in "brain-on" mode, as my colleague Stefan Roock puts it. It's a simple tool that is designed to stimulate conversation and facilitate investigation. Choose the time window carefully, and decide whether to take into account all sprints or just a subset. Know whether or not any sprints show anomalies that might distort the forecast—for instance, team members falling sick, a server crash halting development, or the team making exceptional progress—and adjust the trend line accordingly.

By the way, my favorite tool for creating, updating, and storing the burndown chart is a sheet of flip-chart paper, as it facilitates dialogue and collaboration. And it avoids the illusion of accuracy that electronic reports can portray. Whatever the tool, it's a good idea to display the chart in the team room and bring it along to the sprint review meeting.

The Release Burndown Bar

A more sophisticated version of the release burndown chart is the release burndown bar (Cohn 2005, 221–24). The release burndown bar has all the properties of the release burndown chart but differentiates between reestimating items and burning effort on the one hand, and adding and removing product backlog items on the other. If the team makes progress or reduces its estimates, the top of the bar moves down. If the team increases its estimates, the top of the bar moves up. If new items are added to the backlog, the bottom moves down; if items are taken out of the backlog or are replaced with lower-effort ones, the bottom moves up. Figure 4.2 shows a sample release burndown bar.

The release burndown bar in Figure 4.2 paints the same picture as the sample burndown chart in Figure 4.1. The difference is that we now better understand what happened in sprints three and four. The top of the bars moving down tells us that the team made progress in both sprints. The fact that the bottom of the bar moved down in sprint three tells us that new items were added to the backlog. In sprint four, the bottom moved up, indicating that items were removed from the backlog. Note that the very first bar

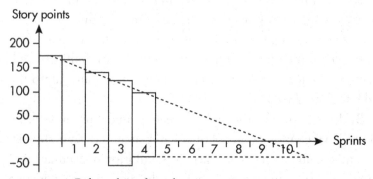

FIGURE 4.2 Release burndown bar

states the amount of work prior to the first sprint. There are two dashed trend lines in Figure 4.2, a lower and an upper one. The upper one represents the burndown trend and is created in the same way as in the release burndown chart. The lower signals the current zero line.

THE RELEASE PLAN

"Plans are nothing; planning is everything," observed Dwight D. Eisenhower. This insight is particularly applicable to the release plan. Although teams are not required to have a release plan in Scrum, they certainly have to plan the release. Many Scrum teams find it sufficient to use a release burndown and to group product backlog items into subsets to indicate which functionality will be delivered in which release.[7] But large Scrum projects, or those that need to coordinate with other projects, partners, or suppliers, will probably want to use a formal plan.

The release plan is like a rough map that guides us to our destination. It forecasts how the product is likely to come to life and when software will be released. A release plan is an advanced version of the release burndown—a burndown on steroids, so to speak. It provides more information than a burndown but is also more complex. The plan is based on four factors: the product backlog items, the remaining effort in the backlog, the velocity, and time. The release plan is by no means fixed. It changes as the product backlog evolves and our understanding of effort and velocity improves. As with the release burndown, the release plan is best created and updated collaboratively in the sprint review meeting.

To get the most out of the plan, I like to show the functionality each release will provide in terms of themes or epics. Showing

---

7. These subsets are also called *release backlogs* (Schwaber and Beedle 2002, 71–72).

stories in the release plan tends to introduce too much detail. (The exception to this rule is on large projects, as I explain later in this chapter.) It's also useful to provide whatever information is necessary to coordinate with others, and to state known changes influencing the velocity, such as a change in the team composition or the project organization. Table 4.2 illustrates a sample release plan.

TABLE 4.2 Sample Release Plan

Sprint	1	2	3	4	5	6	7	8
Velocity forecast	N/A	12–32	18–28	21–28	11–18	16–23	21–28	21–28
Actual velocity	20	25	28					
Dependencies			Imaging library					
Releases				Alpha: Calls, basic text messages	Holidays	Beta: Conference calls, picture messages		V1.0
				Current sprint				

In the example in Table 4.2, the project is currently in the fourth sprint and expects to be able to deliver version 1.0 after four more sprints. Each sprint is two weeks long. An alpha version implementing two themes is released to selected customers after the fourth sprint. A beta version providing two more themes is shipped after the sixth sprint. Although these releases are called *alpha* and *beta*, they are product increments that fulfill the definition of done. Version 1.0 is shipped after eight sprints, or four months. The project expects a supply in the third sprint. The release plan documents the actual velocity and provides a forecast for the remaining sprints.

Forecasting Velocity

To forecast the velocity, we take the following steps: If a new product is being developed, if the team has never worked together, or if its composition has changed significantly, we observe the velocity by carrying out at least one sprint, but preferably two or three sprints. As mentioned before, it can take several sprints for the velocity to stabilize. We can then use the range of observed velocities to forecast the velocity for the remaining sprints. In the release plan in Table 4.2, this would result in a velocity range of 20 to 28 points for the fourth sprint onward with 24 points as the average (mean).

Alternatively, we can use Table 4.3 to anticipate the future velocity (Cohn 2005, 180), as the Scrum team did in the release plan in Table 4.2.

TABLE 4.3 Multipliers for Velocity Based on Number of Sprints Complete*

Sprints Completed	Low Multiplier	High Multiplier
1	0.6	1.60
2	0.8	1.25
3	0.85	1.15
4 or more	0.9	1.10

*From *Agile Estimating and Planning* by Mike Cohn. Reprinted by permission.

Using the average (mean) velocity of the first three sprints in Table 4.2, we multiply 24 by the appropriate low and high multiplier in Table 4.3. This results in a velocity range of 21 to 28 points.

As soon as the team has run five or more sprints, we can create a high-confidence forecast (Cohn 2009, 297–300). Say we are at the end of sprint eight in Table 4.2, and we now want to forecast the team's velocity in the next release. The velocities of the completed sprints are as follows: 20, 25, 28, 26, 16, 20, 26, 26. We now discard any data from sprints that show anomalies, such as half the team falling ill or the integration server being down for several days, if applicable. We then sort the list in ascending order, which results in the following sequence: 16, 20, 20, 25, 26, 26, 26, 28. We can now use Table 4.4 to determine the future velocity with 90% confidence.

TABLE 4.4 Use the nth Lowest and the nth Highest Observation of a Sorted List of Velocities to Find a 90% Confidence Interval*

Number of Velocity Observations	nth Velocity Observation
5	1
8	2
11	3
13	4
16	5
18	6
21	7
23	8
26	9

*From *Succeeding with Agile: Software Development Using Scrum* by Mike Cohn. Reprinted by permission.

Because we have run eight sprints, we pick the second velocity observation from the beginning and the end of the sequence. This gives us a velocity range of 20 to 26 with an average (mean) velocity of 23. We can be 90% confident that the actual velocity will be within this range.

Creating the Release Plan

Once we have forecasted the velocity, we divide the remaining effort in the product backlog by the mean velocity or velocity range, giving us a provisional number of the remaining sprints required. We then map the identified number of sprints onto the calendar and consider the factors that are likely to influence the velocity and that are not accounted for in the velocity forecast. These can include holidays, vacations, training and development, sickness statistics, and planned changes to the project organization, such as modifying the team composition. We adjust the forecasted velocity of each sprint accordingly.

Let's look at the release plan in Table 4.2 again. It states an actual velocity for the first three sprints of 20, 25, and 28. The average (mean) velocity per sprint, then, is 24 points. The Scrum team has forecasted a velocity of 21 to 28 points for the fourth, seventh, and eighth sprints using the multipliers in Table 4.3. The release plan also anticipates a velocity drop in sprints five and six, when several team members will take time off and then return to work.

If the work in the product backlog cannot be delivered within the window of opportunity, assuming it is the launch date that is fixed, we can either reduce the functionality or increase the budget to add people (for instance, a specialist) to the team.

My favorite tool for capturing the release plan is a whiteboard placed in the team room. Some are even equipped with little wheels, making it possible to roll the whole board into a different room. The release plan can, of course, be kept in an electronic tool such as a spreadsheet. Whatever tool is used, though, the plan should create transparency and facilitate dialogue between the Scrum team and stakeholders.

RELEASE PLANNING ON LARGE PROJECTS

Release planning on large projects requires additional practices. These include establishing a common baseline for estimates, performing look-ahead planning, and, if unavoidable, pipelining the work.

Common Baseline for Estimates

When several teams are estimating items in one product backlog, the teams need to agree on a common baseline for their estimates, the range of story points, and the semantics of each number. Otherwise, understanding how much effort is contained in the product backlog will be very difficult. If the project grows organically, common estimates usually emerge. The first team creates the original figures, and these guide the teams that join the project later on. If the project has to employ several teams right from the start, representatives from each of the different teams should hold a joint effort estimation workshop, to agree on a common range with common semantics.

Look-Ahead Planning

Helping each team to succeed while optimizing the progress of the entire project requires some extra work. The first thing we have to do is to look ahead two to three sprints to understand which product backlog items are likely to be worked on (Cohn 2005, 206; Pichler 2008, 146). This requires decomposing and refining product backlog items earlier; more detailed items can now be found at the top of the product backlog.

The next step is to identify any dependencies between the teams by asking the following questions: Do they have to work on the same feature or component? Does any team act as the supplier of another team? If so, is it feasible to supply the feature or component and use it in the same sprint? To eliminate problematic dependencies, we may have to change the product backlog prioritization. For instance, instead of having two teams working on the same subsystem in the next sprint, we may consider postponing some of the requirements to a later sprint and bringing forward other items, thereby adjusting the product backlog prioritization. After resolving any problematic dependencies, we consider the workload generated for each team. Is a team likely to be overworked in the next sprint? Is a team likely to be underutilized? If either is true, we may again go back and change the product backlog prioritization.

We may have to carry out the steps several times to achieve an optimal balance between the needs of the individual teams and those of the overall project. Once that's done, we add the stories to the next two to three sprints in the release plan. Notice that this exercise does not impact the team's empowerment. Anticipating requirements does not mean that the teams will actually commit to them. The consequence of all this is more work. Unfortunately, there is no alternative. Not looking ahead is like running through the woods in the dark without a flashlight or headlamp. Chances are that we will bump against trees and hurt ourselves.

Pipelining

Pipelining is a last resort. You should employ this technique only if all other options have failed. Pipelining separates what belongs together. It spreads the delivery of one product backlog item across multiple sprints (Larman 2004, 251–53). Here is how it works: Say we employ two teams, team A and team B. Team A has to supply a component to team B, and team B has to build on it. As part of our look-ahead planning, we discover that it is not feasible to perform both pieces of work in the same sprint. We also find it difficult to reduce the amount of work by decomposing the requirements further. As a last resort, we pipeline the work. We ask team A to implement the component in the next sprint and team B to extend it in the subsequent one.

This sounds fine, but it presents us with a problem: How much is done once team A has finished its work? And how can we ensure that the component will be working as expected when team B starts to extend it? Since partially done work never earns any points, team A's work is not reflected in the release burndown, making it more difficult to clearly see the progress. To make things worse, feeding buffers may have to be used to ensure that team A is indeed able to supply the component when required (Cohn 2005, 208). A feeding buffer provides a contingency in case team A faces more work to create the component than expected. Using feature teams rather than component teams whenever possible will reduce the need for pipelining.

COMMON MISTAKES

Avoid the following mistakes when carrying out release planning on a Scrum project: not employing a release burndown or a release plan; a passive product owner who is not engaged in the release planning process; big-bang releases, delivering lots of functionality in one go; and compromising quality.

No Release Burndown or Plan

I have seen organizations that were used to creating a detailed project plan up front go to the other extreme and not carry out any release planning at all. Thinking only from sprint to sprint is dangerous—and an easy trap to fall into. Doing so makes it difficult to assess the project's progress and adapt the product and project in the right way. Always have a release burndown or release plan in place. Put it up in the team room and on the project's wiki so it's visible to everyone.

Product Owner in the Passenger Seat

The product owner should be actively involved in the release planning activities and not delegate them to the ScrumMaster or the team. Release planning is as much a collaborative exercise as product backlog grooming. As such, it requires the full participation of the product owner. In fact, the product owner should drive the release planning activities. As the person first and foremost responsible for the success of the product, it is in the best interest of the product owner to guide the project proactively.

Big-Bang Release

If there is one piece of advice you take away from this chapter, do everything you can to release software early and frequently. Avoid a big-bang release—shipping the product only after all the functionality has been implemented. This makes it difficult, if not impossible, to incorporate feedback from customers and users and reduces the likelihood of creating a product people love. And there is another drawback. A big-bang release means that the team deploys the software for the first time when it's time to launch. This often puts stress on the team members and can result in a missed launch date.

Quality Compromises

The product owner might be tempted to release more functionality by sacrificing quality. After all, it could have been a common way of achieving faster progress in the past. Cut a few corners here and there, do a little less testing, and delay creating some documentation. The problem is that compromising quality leaves teams with a product that is more difficult and expensive to maintain and extend. Yes, the team gets more done now. But it will get less done in a few months' time. Cutting quality also makes it difficult for the team to take pride in its work. It undermines craftsmanship and good engineering practices. Teams must have a definition of done in place that states the criteria product increments must fulfill, and the product owner must apply the criteria at each sprint review; no partially done or defective work can be accepted. Simplify release planning by timeboxing your projects and establish a steady innovation cadence.

REFLECTION

Why wait for the official product launch to see how the market responds? Release early and often, but with high quality. Learn from early customer and user feedback and incorporate it into the software. Get it out. Then get it right.

What would be the consequences of fixing time and quality and flexing functionality?

What would be the benefits to releasing early and frequently? And what would it take to do it?

What would it take to organize your projects in quarterly cycles?

What's the velocity of your team?

Do you employ a release burndown or plan? Who creates and updates it?

5

• • •

COLLABORATING IN THE SPRINT MEETINGS

It's a myth that artists just wait to be struck by ingenious ideas and then effortlessly turn them into amazing masterpieces. The truth is that innovation requires dedication, hard work, and discipline. Take the renowned American painter and photographer Chuck Close. His trademark technique is to paint from photographs, dividing his canvas into tiny squares and filling each with little squiggles that are analogous to pixels. Viewers see the individual shapes up close, but as they back away, the image gels into a portrait. Close explains how he works (Oberkirch 2008):

> My paintings are built incrementally, one unit at a time, in a way that's not all that different than the way, say, a writer would work.... One of the nice things [about] working incrementally is that I don't have to reinvent the wheel every single day. Today I did what I did. You can pick it up and put it down. I don't have to wait for inspiration. There are no good days or bad days. Every day essentially builds positively on what I did the day before.

Luckily, Scrum provides the means to work incrementally, to bring the product to life step by step, each sprint building on the results of the previous ones. Sprints are structured by meetings. The sprint planning meeting starts the sprint, the Daily Scrum provides a steady rhythm throughout the iteration, and the sprint review and retrospective close the cycle. The meetings are a valuable opportunity to interact and connect, to share and collaborate. Gerry Laybourne, product owner of Ript, a visual planning software, agrees (Judy 2007):

> In the year it took us to build [Ript], I only missed one of our every other week meetings. I didn't miss these meeting[s] for the best reason: they were truly fun because I learned so much.

This chapter is specifically for product owners. I want to talk directly to you about your involvement in the Scrum meetings and provide tips for collaborating with the team effectively.

SPRINT PLANNING

The sprint planning meeting allows the team to plan its work and commit to a sprint goal, thereby laying the foundation for its self-organization. As the product owner, your responsibility is to make sure the product backlog is well groomed—its items prioritized and its high-priority items detailed—prior to the sprint planning meeting. You will also be expected to attend the sprint planning meeting in order to clarify requirements and answer questions.

Your role during sprint planning is to help the team understand *what* must be done. The team figures out *how much* can be done and *how* to do it. You are not authorized to tell the team how much work should be pulled into the sprint or to identify tasks on behalf of the team. These are solely the team's responsibility. And the team should commit to only as much work as it can realistically deliver. Limiting the amount of work per sprint to the team's capacity and capability creates a *sustainable pace*: "The sponsors, developers, and users should be able to maintain a constant pace indefinitely" (Beck et al. 2001). There is little benefit in trying to achieve an overly ambitious goal in one sprint only to be exhausted in the next one. Scrum favors a smooth, steady flow of work from the product backlog into the sprints. Reliability is more valuable than false ambition; it is the prerequisite for making realistic forecasts. And too much pressure kills playfulness and hampers creativity.

Be aware that a commitment is not a guarantee. It can take a new team two to three sprints to learn how to make commitments it can meet. Plus, software development is full of unknowns; uncertainty and risk go hand in hand with innovation. As Murphy's Law states, "Everything that can possibly go wrong will go wrong." Risks can materialize; problems might not always get resolved quickly. Failing to reach the sprint goal happens—but it should be an exception. If it does happen, use the sprint retrospective to uncover the root cause and to identify improvement measures.

DEFINITION OF DONE

How does the team know that work is *done*? And how can you, as the product owner, decide whether an item has been successfully completed? The solution is to agree on the definition of done—a description of the criteria every increment must fulfill. The done criteria typically require that product backlog items be transformed into working software that is thoroughly tested and adequately documented. Requirements are consequently implemented, tested, and documented in the same sprint. The exception to this is visioning sprints, where the goal is not to build shippable software but to generate relevant knowledge so that a product vision is available. Those sprints have their own unique definition of done.

Prior to the first sprint, you should meet with the ScrumMaster and team to create a definition of done that includes the properties every increment must fulfill. Some projects I have worked with have included specific targets in their definitions of done—for instance, the unit test coverage required. Once you all agree on the definition, it should be written down and kept visible throughout the project.

DAILY SCRUM

The Daily Scrum allows the team to manage its work and to uncover impediments on a daily basis. As the product owner, you should attend the meeting whenever possible. It's a great opportunity to understand the progress being made and to see if the team needs help (for instance, you might need to answer questions, review work results, or help remove impediments). You can also share information and update the team on what you have been working on and are planning to do next. Your work often provides valuable information about the activities at the release level and the project periphery.

When attending the Daily Scrum, be careful not to interfere with the team's self-organization. Do not identify or assign tasks, and do not make any comments on the progress achieved by individuals—out loud or through body language. If you are concerned about the progress, share your view in a constructive manner, perhaps by asking questions.[1] If you are worried about meeting the sprint goal, for instance, you can say, "I noticed that the sprint burndown shows a lot of work left to do. Is that something of concern to you?" By asking questions, you raise the team's awareness but leave it up to the team to act.

Impediments

Untreated problems proliferate like mushrooms in the dark. That's why Scrum puts an emphasis on impediments management—recognizing and treating problems that impede progress and harm

---

1. Asking questions to communicate information is also referred to as the Socratic method. It dates back to the ancient Greek philosopher Socrates, who famously used questions to teach philosophy.

the project. Team members raise impediments in the Daily Scrum, and the ScrumMaster ensures that they are resolved as quickly as possible. Even though dealing with problems can seem to slow down the project, it avoids bigger issues and bigger delays later on. "Problems are treasures," writes lean management expert Pascal Dennis. "They provide an opportunity to learn and improve" (2006, 19).

SPRINT BACKLOG AND SPRINT BURNDOWN

The sprint backlog comprises all activities necessary to reach the sprint goal. The team creates the sprint backlog in the sprint planning meeting and updates it on a regular basis, at least once per day. During these updates, the team might add new activities or remove redundant ones; the team also records the effort left for each task. I prefer to work with a task board that is placed in the team room, visible to everyone. The sprint burndown chart allows the team to understand its progress and the likelihood of meeting the sprint goal. The team can then adapt its work accordingly.

The sprint backlog and sprint burndown primarily serve the team, as they facilitate self-organization. The artifacts can certainly help you, as the product owner, determine whether the team is likely to deliver on its commitment, but neither is intended as a reporting mechanism to stakeholders. If stakeholders, such as customers and management, are interested in the progress within the sprint, they are welcome to attend the Daily Scrum as silent observers and the sprint review meetings as active participants.

SPRINT REVIEW

The sprint review meeting facilitates developing a successful product. It gives the Scrum team a chance to collaborate with the stakeholders, an opportunity to investigate the product's actual development to date and decide on a way forward—rather than assuming that everything is going according to plan. The stakeholders can include representatives from marketing, sales, and service, as well as customers and users. I vividly remember a conversation with a customer of Primavera Systems, Inc., a provider of project, program, and portfolio management software solutions, who attended the company's sprint reviews. He found the meetings extremely valuable, loved the transparency, and appreciated the opportunity to influence the development of the product. Note that the prep work for the meeting should be kept to a minimum. The meeting should be low-key, and not a show. Teams should refrain from giving a formal presentation and avoid using slides. The purpose of the meeting is not to impress or to create excitement but to provide transparency, and to inspect and adapt the product.

As the product owner, your job is to kick off the meeting by comparing the product increment to the sprint goal, the actual to the target, in order to determine the progress. Make sure you thoroughly review the product increment and accept or reject each product backlog item to which the team has committed. The best way to do this is to grab the keyboard and run a few tests. Don't forget: Accept only product backlog items that comply with the definition of done and, if user stories are used, fulfill the acceptance criteria. Never accept unfinished or defective items. These earn zero points and are put back into the product backlog. Note that carrying an inventory of partially done work clouds progress and leads to anomalies in the release burndown chart.

Always give a clear and constructive message to the team when you provide feedback. Honor the team's effort and goodwill. Be honest and straight. If you are pleased with what has been achieved, praise the team. If you are disappointed, say so. While giving feedback, remember that delivering the sprint goal is a team effort. As such, always address the entire team, rather than singling out individuals. Show respect to your fellow Scrum team members, be aware of your intentions and actions, and ask yourself how you can help the team move forward.[2]

---

2. Respect is so important in Scrum that it forms one of its five values (Schwaber and Beedle 2002, 147–54). The other four are commitment, focus, openness, and courage.

Once the progress has been determined, ask the stakeholders for feedback on the product increment. Do they like what they see? How does the product have to be adapted to make it a success? Is the vision still valid? Is functionality missing or is there too much functionality? Is a feature implemented incorrectly? Should the look and feel be adjusted? If so, why? It is not unusual to discover new requirements now or to find out that product backlog items have become redundant. Note that the stakeholder feedback allows you and the team to see the increment through their eyes, mitigating the danger of groupthink. To receive great feedback, manage stakeholder expectations. Explain that an early product increment might bear only a slight resemblance to the final product, that new ideas and requirements should support the vision, and that stakeholders might have to wait one or two sprints before these new ideas can be implemented, depending on the priority and the grooming effort.

Just-in-Time Reviews

As the product owner, you don't have to wait until the sprint review meeting to provide feedback on work results. It's often helpful to carry out just-in-time reviews as the results emerge in the sprint. This gives the team an opportunity during the sprint to adjust the results, if necessary. Just-in-time reviews work best when the product backlog items pulled into the sprint are small enough that the team can complete them within a few days.

SPRINT RETROSPECTIVE

Sprint retrospectives allow the Scrum team to inspect how the work is carried out, to identify problems and their causes, and to discover improvement measures that will make the work more enjoyable and effective. There is a German proverb that nicely summarizes the central idea of retrospectives: *Selbsterkenntnis ist der erste Schritt zur Besserung*, which means "Reflection is the first step toward improvement."

As the product owner, participate in the sprint retrospective on a regular basis. Attending the meeting allows you to contribute improvement measures and to strengthen the relationship with the rest of the Scrum team. I remember one particular sprint retrospective at one of my clients. The sprint review meeting revealed a mismatch in expectations between the product owner and the team. As a consequence, the product owner rejected most of the deliverables. The team members were upset, believing they had done a good job, and the product owner felt let down by the team. We used the subsequent sprint retrospective to clear the air and to analyze what had happened, digging down to the root cause. By constructively discussing the situation, the Scrum team managed to identify two important improvement measures: The product owner would try to spend more time with the team, and the team members would help the product owner groom the product backlog. Without the product owner's presence at the retrospective, the team would have struggled to identify the right measures.

Making sustained improvements requires team members to recognize that even the best teams can get better, to focus on what's holding back the team most, and to unearth the underlying causes. All improvement measures have to be actionable and should usually be implemented in the next sprint. If bigger improvements, such as purchasing and installing a new build server, are needed, they are added to the product backlog.

SPRINT MEETINGS ON LARGE PROJECTS

Although large projects follow the Scrum meeting schedule, the meetings have to be adapted. This section discusses the necessary adjustments.

Joint Sprint Planning

Conducting a sprint planning meeting with multiple teams requires additional prep work. This includes extending the grooming horizon and carrying out look-ahead planning as described in Chapter 3 and Chapter 4. I have found that large projects often benefit from the teams—or at least team representatives—coming together at the start of the sprint planning meeting to discuss and understand the overarching sprint goal to which all teams contribute. Once the teams have conducted their individual sprint planning activities, it is useful for the teams to reconvene again to learn what the entire project plans to achieve in the sprint.

Scrum of Scrums

The Scrum of Scrums meeting allows multiple teams to coordinate on a daily basis throughout the sprint. Team representatives meet following their teams' Daily Scrums to discuss the status quo, the work planned, and any dependencies between the teams (Schwaber 2007, 72). Note that this meeting is tactical in nature. It cannot compensate for a lack of sprint prep work, such as look-ahead planning.

Joint Sprint Review

Having an effective sprint review meeting with one or two teams plus customers, management, and other stakeholders is challenging enough. With five, ten, or more teams, it's even more difficult to ensure a common understanding of the progress and to decide on the way forward. Primavera found a great way to manage its sprint review meetings, which often involved as many as 15 teams. Bob Schatz, former vice president of development at Primavera, explains: "Our sprint reviews could best be described as being like science fairs at school. Each team set up a station where they demonstrated what they worked on. The end users, stakeholders, and a few others from our company formed small teams. Each reviewer team started at a different station. We ran 15-minute iterations moving reviewer teams from station to station. It was an environment of high-energy, excitement, and fun" (Schatz 2009).[3] Getting the teams and stakeholders together in one room is a great way to allow everyone to interact and to share. If that's not possible in the company's buildings, consider using an alternative location, such as a conference venue, at least for every other review meeting.

Joint Sprint Retrospective

Teams still benefit from having their own sprint retrospectives and from implementing their own improvement measures on a large Scrum project. But that's not enough. For optimal results, the teams should identify common improvement measures and share their mutual insights. Joint sprint retrospectives allow the teams to do this. An efficient way to hold a joint retrospective is involving team representatives. This fosters cross-team pollination, but it does not leverage the creativity and knowledge of all project members. The alternative is a joint retrospective with all teams. Such a retrospective is costly—it can take half a day or longer—but it uses the teams' collective wisdom and allows all team members to interact, thereby strengthening inter-team relationships. A great way to manage a joint retrospective is to use Open Space Technology (Owen 1997), where the project members self-organize around problem areas and identify improvement measures. Note that the two options can be happily combined. An organization might choose, for instance, to have meetings of team representatives as the default and also to employ a joint retrospective with all teams present after every third sprint.

---

3. Note that the product owners helped present the work results to the reviewers.

COMMON MISTAKES

As the product owner, you can foster a close and trustful collaboration with the ScrumMaster and team by avoiding these common mistakes: bungee product owner, passive product owner, unsustainable pace, smoke and mirrors, and reporting up the sprint burndown.

The Bungee Product Owner

A bungee product owner appears at sprint planning, vanishes, and then reemerges at the sprint review meeting. A bungee product owner has limited or no collaboration with the team during the sprint; even reaching the individual via telephone or email can be difficult. Sometimes the ScrumMaster or a team member fills the void and acts as a proxy product owner, which allows the team to move forward but fails to resolve the underlying causes of the problem. As the product owner, you are vital to the success of the product. As such, your product owner responsibilities must be your number-one priority. You should spend enough time on-site with the team, making yourself available to answer questions, review work, or remove impediments.

The Passive Product Owner

The team room was crowded. The product owner, ScrumMaster, team, users, and a few line managers were watching a computer screen. The tester in front of the computer was doing his best to explain the functionality he was demoing. The product owner looked rather uncomfortable, his body ever so slowly edging away from the screen. Every now and then he would nod and say, "OK." After ten minutes, the demo was over. The ScrumMaster looked at the product owner and asked, "Are you happy with what you have seen?" The product owner nodded once more and said, "Good job." He then stood up and left the room. The other Scrum team members looked at each other in silence. "Time to start the retro," said the ScrumMaster.

I wish I had fabricated this little story. I wish even more that I had witnessed it only once. Unfortunately, I have seen product owners acting as passive bystanders in sprint review meetings many times. But the meeting is not a show for you to go and watch. Its objective is to figure out together what needs to be done to maximize the chances of creating a successful product. As a product owner, you must actively contribute to the meeting to ensure the product is evolving in the right way.

Unsustainable Pace

"There is no break between sprints. The new sprint starts on the next business day," I explain. An attendee raises her hand and asks, "But how does the team recover?" "They don't," I answer. I look into bleak faces; some people shake their heads. I continue: "You have to make sure that the team is empowered to take on the right amount of work—only as many product backlog items as they can realistically transform into a product increment, without getting worn out, without being overworked."

Developing a product is like running a marathon. If you want to finish, you have to choose a steady pace. Many product owners make the mistake of pressuring the team to take on more work. This may achieve a short-term velocity increase but is not sustainable. In fact, it is counterproductive. Sprints turn into mini death marches; people will burn out quickly, fall ill, or leave. As the product owner, you must respect the team's empowerment—no matter what the release burndown looks like. If the progress is too slow, get everyone together to search for a creative, healthy solution rather than bullying people into working longer hours.

Smoke and Mirrors

One of my favorite childhood memories is visiting the local fun fair, with its rides and shows. One attraction impressed me particularly: a maze with walls made out of mirrors projecting strange images and creating deceiving illusions. A sprint review meeting where colorful slides are shown or where the team presents results not corresponding to the definition of done is its own maze. We can't see things for what they are; we are lost in an illusion. It's all about the show—smoke and mirrors. To create transparency, encourage teams to keep sprint review meetings real—no matter who is in the room. (Teams are allowed to demo only work results that they believe correspond to the definition of done.)

Reporting Up the Sprint Burndown

Some companies use the sprint burndown as a project report in status meetings or as a document for senior management. Both are a misuse of the artifact. Its primary purpose is to help the team inspect its progress on a daily basis and adapt its work accordingly. It is not a status report. Using the sprint burndown as a reporting tool turns it into a control mechanism. Requests from management for regular views into the sprint burndown are a telltale sign of a lack of trust. As the product owner, you can help resolve the situation by inviting stakeholders to the sprint review meetings and the Daily Scrums. And use only the *release* burndown or the release plan to communicate progress. (If the underlying problem is that more inspect and adapt opportunities are needed, the team should consider shortening the sprint length.)

REFLECTION

As the product owner, you guide and influence the team. Your behavior matters. A lot. Frequently reflect on your intentions and actions. Be a team player. Be open and supportive. At the same time, be firm and don't shy away from providing difficult feedback in the sprint meetings. The following questions will help you reflect on your behavior:

> *How can you support the team in the sprint planning meeting without violating the team's self-organization?*
>
> *How can you effectively contribute to the Daily Scrum?*
>
> *How can you closely collaborate with the team to provide early feedback on work results?*
>
> *How can you make your sprint review meetings even more effective and fun?*
>
> *Do you attend the sprint retrospectives? If not, what would it take to attend them? What would be the benefits?*

6
. . .

TRANSITIONING INTO THE PRODUCT OWNER ROLE

When I met Paul, a first-time product owner, he asked me, "What do I really have to do and how much time will it require?" Paul explained that he wanted to double-check his day-to-day responsibilities. He was especially worried about the time commitment he had to make and the support he would get from his boss. Paul is not unique. Many new product owners are not clear about their responsibilities and are unsure how to best transition into their new role. Being a first-time product owner can be challenging, and it often requires personal and organizational changes. These changes can be difficult, even painful at times. This chapter speaks directly to readers transitioning into the role and to managers guiding a Scrum adoption. You can find a more comprehensive description of Scrum transition practices in Schwaber (2007) and Cohn (2009).

BECOMING A GREAT PRODUCT OWNER

Becoming a great product owner takes time and requires dedication. This section helps readers transition into and get better at playing the role.

Know Yourself

The first step to becoming a great product owner is to understand who you are and how you hope to develop professionally. Reflect on your skills and abilities and compare them to the responsibilities of the product owner; identify the aspects of the role you are likely to find difficult and that you may struggle with.

As I mentioned in Chapter 1, the product owner role is multi-faceted. It's difficult—perhaps impossible—to find new product owners who have every necessary skill. You can therefore expect to find gaps in your own knowledge and skills. John, for instance, has a lot of expertise in interacting with customers and creating product road maps but lacks the skills to write good user stories and to create a release plan. Jane, on the other hand, has plenty of experience in writing requirements and is familiar with release planning but lacks visioning skills. Both will need to emphasize their strengths and shore up their weaknesses. Lyssa Adkins, author of *Coaching Agile Teams*, gives the advice shown in Table 6.1 to new product owners.[1]

TABLE 6.1 Product Owner Dos and Don'ts

Do	Don't
Say *what* needs to get done.	Say *how* to do it or *how much* it will take.
Challenge the team.	Bully the team.
Get interested in building a high-performance team.	Focus on the short-term deliveries only.
Practice business-value-driven thinking.	Stick to the original scope and approach "no matter what."
Protect the team from outside noise.	Worry the team with changes that might happen, until they become real.
Incorporate change between sprints.	Allow change to creep into sprints.

---

1. Personal communication with Lyssa Adkins, June 29, 2009.

Develop and Grow

Understanding where your greatest development potential lies allows you to select the right training measures. Product-owners-to-be usually benefit from attending a Scrum product owner training course to quickly acquire the relevant knowledge. But it's not all about information. As a new product owner, embrace the agile work ethos and start to live the Scrum values: Be committed to the product and the team, focus on the product owner job, be open and encourage transparency, show respect to the people with whom you interact, and have the courage to do the right thing and to act in the right way (Schwaber and Beedle 2002, 147–54). Be a team player, and trust your fellow Scrum team members.

Give yourself time to grow into the role. It's unrealistic to expect to do a perfect job right from the start; making mistakes is often part of the learning process. Be patient but never complacent. Once you have started working as a product owner, you will be able to see your strengths and weaknesses more clearly. Use the sprint retrospective to receive feedback from the ScrumMaster and team on your own performance and adapt accordingly.

Get a Coach

In addition to attending a training course and reading books on Scrum, first-time product owners greatly benefit from coaching. A coach acts like a mirror, allowing new product owners to see the impact of their words and actions more clearly. Take Paul, the product owner from the beginning of the chapter. When I started coaching Paul, he was not used to working closely with development teams. He felt particularly uncomfortable in the sprint review meetings and would either provide rather harsh feedback or be unnaturally quiet. Paul was not aware of this behavior until I pointed it out to him. After I brought the issue to Paul's attention, we explored how he could help make the review meetings more effective and enjoyable for everyone. One particularly helpful tenet for Paul was to *be tough on the problem but easy on the people*. After our discussion, Paul started to tackle issues in a constructive way and to openly recognize the goodwill and effort of the team.

Another coaching form that works very well is an apprenticeship model. Take the example of one of my clients. Sarah, the head of a business unit, took on the product owner role for the first release of a new product. She quickly realized that she would not have enough time to be a product owner in the long term. Shortly after the start of the project, Sarah involved one of her staff members, Tom, as an assistant. This gave Tom time to learn the ropes. Once the first release had been deployed successfully, Sarah was able to smoothly pass on the product owner role to Tom.

Ensure That You Have Sponsorship from the Right Level

To work effectively as a product owner, you rely on management's continued trust and support. Depending on the organization and situation, the right level of management might be the vice president of product management, the head of the business unit, the leadership team, or the CEO. To get the necessary management attention and support, you might have to educate management about the importance of your role and the extent of its authority and responsibility. Without sponsorship from the right level, you are likely to lack authority and, as a consequence, will struggle to do a good job.

You're Not Done Yet

After a few months working in your new role and with the initial hurdles cleared, you are likely to feel more settled. Getting to that stage is great, but don't stop there. Continue to grow and develop by regularly reflecting on your work. Listen to feedback from your fellow Scrum team members, and work on the remaining gaps in knowledge or skills. A great way to improve is to join a product

owner community, where you can connect with other product owners, exchange ideas and experiences, share insights, and identify
best practices, for instance, from regular product owner workshops.[2]

DEVELOPING GREAT PRODUCT OWNERS

While each individual product owner needs to assume responsibility for doing a great job, there are a number of things managers guiding a Scrum adoption can do to create an environment that
encourages product owners to flourish. This section describes what
you, as a leader or manager, should do to ensure that this happens.

Recognize the Importance of the Role

Senior managers must recognize the authority and responsibility of
the product owner role and the likely impact it is going to have on
the organization. Doing so is not only crucial for making agile product management work, but it is also a critical success factor for any
Scrum adoption. Ken Schwaber agrees (2007, 85):

> Until recently, I viewed this relationship [between product
> management and development] as one of many changes
> in a Scrum adoption. I now view it as the most critical
> change, the lynchpin of the adoption. If this change is suc-
> cessful, the use of Scrum will persist and benefits will
> increase. If the change isn't successful, the use of Scrum in
> your enterprise might well unravel.

Select the Right Product Owners

Product owners must be selected with care. As a manager, you must
take into account not only the desirable characteristics of a product
owner (as described in Chapter 1) but also other factors including

---

2. Cohn (2009, 70–79) discusses improvement communities to foster the adoption
of Scrum in more detail.

the product, the domain, and the project size. The best product owner for one product might therefore be less suitable for another one. Additionally, each company has to find its own way to staff the product owner role. At Salesforce.com, for instance, the product managers work as product owners and belong to the same department. At mobile.de the product owner role is staffed with members from the business units; each business unit looks after a set of products or product features.[3] As with anything in Scrum, the proof is in the pudding. Once an organization has run a number of Scrum projects, a common approach to staffing the product owner role usually starts to emerge.

Empower and Support the Product Owners

First-time product owners need time, trust, and support to grow into their new role. Chances are that a new product owner will make mistakes, ranging from not involving stakeholders to interrupting the sprint; it's often part and parcel of the learning process. As a senior manager, you can help flatten the learning curve by providing the right training and coaching measures. "Early immersion and training of the product owners in agile principles, product backlog creation, user story design and estimation and planning is key to the success of any agile team. Also, beyond initial training, continuous product owner coaching throughout the rollout is necessary to ingrain the new process into the culture," write Fry and Greene about their experience at Salesforce.com. They also advise companies to "get professional help. External coaches have done it before and will see the roadblocks coming before you do. They can also help you learn from other organizations that have gone through similar transitions" (2007, 139).

---

3. Personal communication with Brett Queener, senior vice president, products, at Salesforce.com, on June 9, 2009, and with Philip Missler, CTO at mobile.de, on June 18, 2009.

Besides giving product owners adequate training, you can help by empowering the product owners and by ensuring that product owners have enough time to do their job well. A product owner who is not empowered to decide if a feature will be delivered as part of the release, for example, quickly loses credibility among the Scrum team members and the stakeholders. Be aware that working as a product owner is usually a full-time job. The project will suffer if the individual playing the role is overworked. Freeing product owners from their other obligations gives them the ability to pay full attention to their projects.

Sustain the Application of the Product Owner Role

Sustaining product ownership requires developing the necessary organizational capabilities to grow and to develop product owners. This goes beyond injecting initial knowledge into the organization. It includes creating a comprehensive development program and establishing a product owner community. A great way to create such a development program is to base it on the product owners' collective wisdom and to actively involve product owners in its creation, for instance, by holding regular product owner workshops to identify best practices and improvement measures.

Sometimes organizational changes are necessary to fully establish the product owner role. Take the example of CSG Systems, a customer interaction management company that provides software-based solutions. Mauricio Zamora, executive director at CSG, explains the company's approach (Leffingwell 2009):

> We first educated everyone on the differences between the traditional Product Management, agile Product Owner and Architect roles. We then had to convince management that the Product Owner role required dedicated focus. The visibility agile provides made the increasingly obvious gaps in Product Ownership easier to see and address. Finally, we had to revisit and revise organizational titles

and compensation because the new Product Owner role
didn't map well into our existing organization.

Additional changes include creating new career paths and adjusting existing ones, modifying employee selection criteria, creating new development programs, and, for some companies, introducing new organizational structures.

REFLECTION

Applying the product owner role effectively is not only the cornerstone of making agile product management work. It is also a learning process for the individuals playing the role and for the organization. The following questions will help those transitioning to the product owner role:

What are the aspects of the role you are likely to find difficult?

How can you acquire the necessary knowledge to be off to a good start?

Who can help you develop and grow as a product owner?

Are there other product owners in your company you can connect with?

Senior managers play a vital role in choosing and developing product owners and also in championing the Scrum adoption. Leaders, therefore, should explore the following questions to establish the product owner role in their organizations:

How is the product owner role likely to impact the organization?

What are the things that matter most for successful product owners?

How can you help product owners do a great job?

How can the company sustain the effective application of the product owner role?

REFERENCES

37Signals. 2006. *Getting Real: The Smarter, Faster, Easier Way to Build a Successful Web Application*. https://gettingreal. 37signals.com/.

Anthony, Scott D., Mark W. Johnson, Joseph V. Sinfield, and Elizabeth J Altman. 2008. *The Innovator's Guide to Growth: Putting Disruptive Innovations to Work*. Harvard Business School Press.

Beck, Kent. 2000. *Extreme Programming Explained: Embrace Change*. Addison-Wesley.

Beck, Kent, and Cynthia Andres. 2005. *Extreme Programming Explained: Embrace Change*, 2nd edition. Addison-Wesley.

Beck, Kent, and Martin Fowler. 2000. *Planning Extreme Programming*. Addison-Wesley.

Beck, Kent, et al. 2001. The Manifesto for Agile Software Development. http://agilemanifesto.org/ and http://agilemani-festo.org/principles.html.

Brooks, Frederick P. 1995. *The Mythical Man-Month: Essays on Software Engineering*, 2nd edition. Addison-Wesley.

Bryson, John M. 2004. "What to Do When Stakeholders Matter: Stakeholder Identification and Analysis Techniques." *Public Management Review* 6, no. 1, 21–53.

Carroll, Lewis. 1998. *Alice's Adventures in Wonderland and Through the Looking-Glass*. Penguin Classics. (Carroll's *Alice's Adventures in Wonderland* was first published in 1865.)

Catmull, Ed. 2008. "How Pixar Fosters Collective Creativity." *Harvard Business Review*, September, 64–72.

Christensen, Clayton M. 1997. *The Innovator's Dilemma: When Technologies Cause Great Firms to Fail*. Harvard Business School Press.

Cockburn, Alistair. 2005. *Crystal Clear: A Human-Powered Methodology for Small Teams*. Addison-Wesley.

Cohn, Mike. 2004. *User Stories Applied: For Agile Software Development*. Addison-Wesley.

———. 2005. *Agile Estimating and Planning*. Prentice Hall.

———. 2008. "Writing the Product Backlog Just Enough and Just in Time." Scrum Alliance Weekly Column, February 12. www.scrumalliance.org/articles/87-writing-the-product-backlog-just-enough-and-just-in-time.

———. 2009. *Succeeding with Agile: Software Development Using Scrum*. Addison-Wesley.

Conway, Melvin E. 1968. "How Do Committees Invent?" *Datamation*, April, 28–31.

Cooper, Alan. 1999. *The Inmates Are Running the Asylum: Why High-Tech Products Drive Us Crazy and How to Restore Sanity*. Sams Publishing.

Cooper, Robert G. 2001. *Winning at New Products: Accelerating the Process from Idea to Launch*, 3rd edition. Perseus.

Cunningham, Ward. 1992. "The WyCash Portfolio Management System." OOPSLA 1992 Experience Report. http://c2.com/doc/oopsla92.html.

DeMarco, Tom, Peter Hruschka, Tim Lister, Suzanne Robertson, James Robertson, and Steve McMenamin. 2008. *Adrenaline

Junkies and Template Zombies: Understanding Patterns of Project Behavior. Dorset House.

Denne, Mark, and Jane Cleland-Huang. 2004. *Software by Numbers: Low-Risk, High-Return Development*. Sun Microsystems Press.

Dennis, Pascal. 2006. *Getting the Right Things Done: A Leader's Guide to Planning and Execution*. Lean Enterprise Institute.

Finkelstein, Sydney, Andrew Campbell, and Jo Whitehead. 2009. *Think Again: Why Good Leaders Make Bad Decisions and How to Keep It from Happening to You*. Harvard Business School Press.

Fry, Chris, and Steve Greene. 2007. "Large Scale Agile Transformation in an On-Demand World." Paper presented at AGILE 2007, August 13–17, IEEE, 136–42.

Gilb, Tom. 1988. *Principles of Software Engineering Management*. Addison-Wesley.

Girard, Bernard. 2009. *The Google Way: How One Company Is Revolutionizing Management as We Know It*. No Starch Press.

Greene, Steve, and Chris Fry. 2008. "Year of Living Dangerously: How Salesforce.com Delivered Extraordinary Results through a 'Big-Bang' Enterprise Agile Revolution." Presentation at the Scrum Gathering, Chicago, April.

Highsmith, Jim. 2009. *Agile Project Management: Creating Innovative Products*, 2nd edition. Addison-Wesley.

Judy, Ken H. 2007. "CEO and Team: Collective Product Ownership at Oxygen Media." Presentation at the Scrum Gathering, London, November.

Kaner, Sam, Lenny Lind, Catherine Toldi, Sarah Fisk, and Duane Berger. 1996. *Facilitator's Guide to Participatory Decision-Making*. New Society Publishers.

Kano, Noriaki. 1984. "Attractive Quality and Must-Be Quality." *Journal of the Japanese Society for Quality Control*, April, 39–48.

Larman, Craig. 2004. *Agile and Iterative Development: A Manager's Guide*. Addison-Wesley.

Larman, Craig, and Bas Vodde. 2009. *Scaling Lean and Agile Development: Thinking and Organizational Tools for Large-Scale Scrum*. Addison-Wesley.

Leffingwell, Dean. 2009. "The Product Owner in the Agile Enterprise." *Agile Journal*, April 6.

Levitt, Theodore. 1960. "Marketing Myopia." *Harvard Business Review* 38, no. 4, 45–56.

Levy, Steven. 2008. "Inside Chrome: The Secret Project to Crush IE and Remake the Web." *Wired*, no. 16 (October). www.wired.com/techbiz/it/magazine/16-10/mf_chrome.

Lidwell, William, Kritina Holden, and Jill Butler. 2003. *Universal Principles of Design*. Rockport Publishers.

Lynn, Gary S., and Richard R. Reilly. 2002. *Blockbusters: The Five Keys to Developing Great New Products*. HarperCollins.

Maeda, John. 2006. *The Laws of Simplicity*. MIT Press.

Mayer, Marissa. 2006. "Nine Lessons Learned about Creativity at Google." Presentation at Stanford University, May.

Moore, Geoffrey A. 2006. *Crossing the Chasm. Marketing and Selling Disruptive Products to Mainstream Customers*, revised edition. Collins Business Essentials.

Newkirk, James, and Robert C. Martin. 2001. *Extreme Programming in Practice*. Addison-Wesley.

Oberkirch, Brian. 2008. "Working in Close." 34 Folders, November. www.43folders.com/2008/01/11/working-close.

Owen, Harrison. 1997. *Open Space Technology: A User's Guide*, 2nd edition. Berrett-Koehler Publishers.

Pichler, Roman. 2008. *Scrum — Agiles Projektmanagement erfolgreich einsetzen*. dpunkt.verlag.

Poppendieck, Mary and Tom. 2003. *Lean Software Development: An Agile Toolkit for Software Development Managers*. Addison-Wesley.

Reinertsen, Donald G. 1997. *Managing the Design Factory: A Product Developer's Toolkit*. Free Press.

Schmidkonz, Christian. 2008. "Product Owner at SAP — A New Job Title Developed." Presentation at ObjektForum, Stuttgart, September.

Schatz, Bob. 2009. "The Sprint Review: Mastering the Art of Feedback." www.scrumalliance.org/articles/124-the-sprint-review-mastering-the-art-of-feedback.

Schwaber, Ken. 2004. *Agile Project Management with Scrum*. Microsoft Press.

———. 2007. *The Enterprise and Scrum*. Microsoft Press.

———. 2009. "Scrum Guide." Scrum Alliance, May.

Schwaber, Ken, and Mike Beedle. 2002. *Agile Software Development with SCRUM*. Prentice Hall.

Senge, Peter M. 2006. *The Fifth Discipline: The Art and Practice of the Learning Organization*, revised and updated edition. Random House.

Simons, Matthew. 2004. "Distributed Agile Development and the Death of Distance." *Cutter Consortium Executive Report, Sourcing and Vendor Relationships* 5, no. 4.

Smith, Preston G., and Guy M. Merritt. 2002. *Proactive Risk Management: Controlling Uncertainty in Product Development*. Productivity Press.

Smith, Preston G., and Donald G. Reinertsen. 1998. *Developing Products in Half the Time: New Rules, New Tools*. John Wiley and Sons.

Sutherland, Jeff. 2005. "Future of Scrum: Parallel Pipelining of Sprints in Complex Projects." *Proceedings of the Agile Development Conference*, 90–102.

Wake, Bill. 2003. "INVEST in Good Stories, and SMART Tasks." www.xp123.com/xplor/xp0308/index.shtml. August.

Womack, James P., and Daniel T. Jones. 2005. *Lean Solutions: How Companies and Customers Can Create Value and Wealth Together*. Simon and Schuster.

INDEX